ARCANUM
OF NINJA TACTICS

LEGACY OF THE SHADOW WARRIOR

Written By
Mark Steven Grove

Publisher
Warrior Quest Media
www.WarriorQuest.com

First Printing
October 2016

ISBN 978-0692789438
ISBN 0-692789-43-X

Illustrator
Matthew White

Photography
Dan Yahnian

FIGHT FROM THE SHADOWS

PROTECT THE INNOCENT

VANISH

— Chronicles of Kurai Kotori

CONTENTS

DEDICATION

It is not often that a teacher acquires the perfect student. Many instructors train those who are physically gifted, those who excel technically, and those with passion for the adventure. But there are very few students who possess all of these qualities who remain devout throughout a lifetime.

Daryl Rolando is such a man.   He was among the initial wave of students who entered my dojo back in 1983 and he was the first student to earn his black belt. He was also the first to receive a martial name, *Ryu Seishin* (dragon spirit), the first to commit this totem on his forearm with an *Irezumi* (tattoo), and the first to be awarded the title *Kenshi* (sword master) given to acknowledge his superior talents with the blade. He was and is the symbol of warrior-hood within the Kurai Kotori family. No matter what level of skill he acquired, how many ranks or titles he has been awarded, he remains devoted to the path with the eagerness of a beginner. Our journey together is far from over, but the fond memories of the road behind us makes me look forward to what lies ahead. It has been an honor and a privilege. — Mark Steven Grove

ACKNOWLEDGMENTS

I must acknowledge many people who have come and gone in my life who have taught me martial lessons, provided inspiration, and offered many other forms of support. These individuals were instrumental on my path.

Shihan Frank Goody, Dai Shihan Dennis G. Palumbo, Professor Wally Jay, Sensei Miguel Serrano, Professor Ronald Duncan, Sensei Daryl Pennington, Shidoshi Ron Van Clief, Ron Balicki, Diana Lee Inosanto, and my big brother Sifu James Lew, who has shown me what true friendship is all about. I must also thank all my students, past and present, who have walked the path with me.

In Memory of
Joshua Shepherd
Tetsu Taka

FOREWORD

To be asked to write a foreword for a book is not something that comes along every day, every year, or even in a lifetime. To write one for this book, this system for which I have dedicated myself to nearly my entire adult life, is an absolute honor.

I could start by going on about the trials and lessons I have experienced over the years. Ramble over what the warrior way has done for my life and for me as a person. Perhaps I should boast over the integrity and effectiveness of this system. Or maybe recall one of a thousand anecdotes that I experienced in my journey with this lifestyle, and how it might relate to your life. Possibly, I could go over all my opinions and feelings about the master martial artist who wrote this book and shaped my life for decades. But no. I thought to myself the most likely person reading my words, and looking to this book for guidance, is someone very new to this art. I remember what it was like when I was in that moment. A wide eyed youngster fascinated by the Japanese Martial traditions and the mystery of the Ninja. I first walked through the front doors of the Kurai Kotori Ryu dojo to see warriors flipping through the air with weapons, bodies moving with precision, people with intense focus, discipline, and an intangible energy that just permeated the room. It was fate that brought me through those doors and I have been chasing my destiny ever since.

There is a duality to a warrior's life. A warrior must train for personal gain. Gains such as skill, strength, security, artistry, and enlightenment. But a warrior must also "give of thyself" absolutely. Duty towards something, or somebody, outside of their own interests is essential. Mr. Grove's duty is to the collective knowledge and legacy of humanity. It is to preserve and honor the lessons of countless warriors who lived and died on the field of battle. In the process, he has stamped his own signature on a body of information that has evolved over hundreds of years. He created a system of learning that is fluid, cohesive, powerful, beautiful, yet frightening at the same time.

I would like you to understand that the body of information you are about to read is not merely a catalog of historical knowledge...it is a living, dynamic, and life changing entity that has affected and shaped the lives of many people. People of which I have been honored to know. None more so than the man who has quite literally spent his entire life refining the art you are going to read about. To say that this book can't contain even a shade of the magnitude of this art is a gross understatement. But what else can be done? An artist must display his art, teach his pupils, and hope that it takes on a life of its own and survives past his days. Such is the nature of Art and Duty.
— Norman Dehm

INTRODUCTION

The author 1979

I came from an era where there was still a mystery behind martial arts, where those seeking knowledge couldn't just google a subject and have access to articles, blogs, and videos. They had to actually make an effort to find a teacher, be accepted by that teacher, and practice diligently without any praise or the desire to attain belt rankings. No agenda, you simply trained to be the best you could be.

That is my story. At a young age I was exposed to the concept of the Ninja by a few masterful teachers, one of the most prolific being Shihan Frank Goody. I met him at a time in my life that was filled with upheaval, he took me under his wing and shared what seemed like limitless knowledge on the subject. His guidance inspired me to reinvent myself, and somewhere along the line, the very beginnings of what would become the Kurai Kotori style was forming. This was not because I was ever seeking to create a style, but because it was a process prescribed by Shihan Goody in an effort to help me organize my thoughts and methods. To better understand that process, we must begin with the name. *Kurai Kotori* was a training name given to me by Shihan

Shihan Frank Goody

Goody. He translated it as "Dark small bird" which was a reflection of my physical size and speed coupled with a reference to the crow, which is symbolic of the Tengu (*crow warriors*) found in Japanese mythology. He also gave me a translation in which the Japanese characters were written in a way that translated as "Dark lone bird" which he said was due to the fact that I, like every man, was solely responsible for creating and managing my own destiny.

Mine was not a journey to solely acquire skills, but a process by which a boy could evolve into a man. Shihan Goody called this an *internal forge*, where the student is either tempered by the experience or consumed by the flames, a philosophy still maintained in the system today. My most memorable times with him were sitting at the bar at a little diner located on a corner of Broadway and Evans in Denver. It was here that he would fill my head so full of concepts I would at times feel overwhelmed. I committed this information to spiral notebook after spiral notebook with quickly written notes, diagrams, and doodles, which have all survived in some form or another in the Kurai Kotori system.

Fighting technique diagrams from Shihan Frank Goody

Of the many diagrams I received, each one represented multiple variants beyond the technique the drawing depicted. Ultimately the 16 diagrams for Ninjutsu shown above had over 60 different applications and it was from here that the majority of the unarmed skills I now teach originated.

Shihan Goody was not only well versed in Ninjutsu, he was a master of many disciplines. Nagai Ryu Jujutsu, Kobudo, Judo, Kung Fu and Yawara. He was especially focused on teaching me weaponry skills. It was here that I flourished. He would provide me with diagrams and ask me to look at the still picture and create a moving image in my head. He expected me to look beyond the *specific* technique to find its hidden possibilities. In essence, he wanted me to "see" the variables in any given technique intuitively.

6 moves from a 47 move hand claw form from Shihan Frank Goody

The art of fighting with stick weapons became one of my signature skills. The three foot staff and small handheld stick were taught in such a way that defied what most would expect of them. Instead of relying solely on the blunt striking aspects, these weapons were also used to apply elite grappling maneuvers and pressing attacks. I was also taught the use of other small weapons that were easily concealed. I was given a tanto (*dagger*) manriki-gusari (*chain*), and juji shaken (*cross shaped throwing blades*). Shihan Goody related that although the Ninja of old used dozens of exotic weapons, it was with these hidden weapons that I would find my most trusted arsenal.

Swordsmanship was another skill that was mandatory to training, but my first sword was *unique* to say the least. Shihan Goody created a blade for me comprised of a thick machete blade fitted with a large square handguard and a handle that was nearly as long as the blade. He gave me this Shinobigatana (*secret sword*) to teach me the difference between the Ninja's sword compared to a Samurai's blade. Instead of being a meticulously forged and crafted masterpiece, he expressed that a Ninja's sword was a tool as much as it was a weapon. Sharp enough to cut flesh yet sturdy enough to chop down a tree. I also constructed a scabbard for this weapon out of oak that was very strong and could be utilized as a secondary weapon. At times I would be handed a Katana (*long sword*) or Wakizashi (*short sword*) and told that the type of sword in my hands did not matter because my intuitive nature with weapons would give me the ability to adapt instinctively regardless of its length, curvature, or design. The unorthodox Shinobigatana and the techniques I was taught with it formed what would evolve into the swordsmanship skills I still teach today.

Koka Shinobigatana design from Shihan Frank Goody

Shihan Goody also gave me a Japanese scroll that depicted symbolized hand gestures that were designed to release my innermost personal power and expressed that the mind must be as strong as the body. We actively practiced meditation focused on the five elemental furies of earth, water, fire, wind, and celestial.

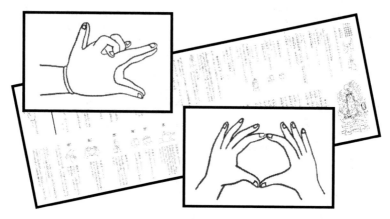

Mystical hand gestures used during meditation

Then In 1983 I was asked by a friend who had visited a dojo in Aurora, Colorado to go over and check out a martial arts supply store connected to the school. When we arrived I met Dennis G. Palumbo, a Hakkoryu Jujutsu master of high renown. During our conversation I mentioned that I practiced Ninjutsu under Shihan Goody and it sparked interest in Shihan Palumbo. He seemed curious about my skills and he asked me to show him some techniques. We went to his training floor and he offered himself up as the recipient of my technique. For about 30 minutes I applied grappling maneuvers and demonstrated kicks and punches and various acrobatic feats. At the end of it all, he said he was very impressed and asked if I would do a demonstration at his studio that he would schedule to occur a few weeks later. I was honored by the request, and before even thinking, I said yes.

What I didn't know was that Shihan Palumbo did a considerable amount of advertising, so when I showed up the morning of this proposed demo, I was shocked that the studio was packed full of people and there were more waiting outside in the parking lot. This was likely due to the recent surge of the Ninja arts in the US. I made my way to the training floor and began the demonstration. Working with both skilled martial artists and random guests invited out onto the floor, I demonstrated both unarmed and weaponry techniques, answered questions through practical application and generally ate up the energy of the room. I found it intoxicating and after that first group left, another was brought in and I started all

The author demonstrating his skills at the Hakkosen Dojo

over again. At the end of it all, I was filled with a type of energy that I had never felt before. But it didn't end there. As I walked up to Shihan Palumbo he handed me a clipboard filled with pages of names. He said all those who signed it were interested in on-going classes. I looked through the pages. These people wanted to train from me? How did this happen. He offered me a mid-week evening time slot to give it a try. Again, I accepted.

The author with mentor Shihan Dennis G. Palumbo

Not only did I start my classes, I was also continuously mentored by Shihan Palumbo and through him had the opportunity to train with many other instructors, including Small Circle Jujutsu Master Professor Wally Jay, who greatly influenced the way I approached grappling techniques.   It was during those early years I refined everything I had learned from Shihan Goody and organized the material into what would become the Kurai Kotori style of Ninjutsu, which was officially recognized under Shihan Palumbo's Hakkoryu Martial Arts Federation.

It was during the mid 80's that I would also begin training the military   rsonnel on Lowry Air Force Base and Fitzsimons   Medical Base, quickly becoming a primary sou   unarmed combatives at both facilities. My classes   d to 6 days a week between all the locations ar   'e to teach students that came from all over the wo

Although K   Ninjutsu is a Gendai system (modern budo   the Meiji Restoration 1866-1869), I still consider   nature due its reliance on the many Koryu (old   concepts taught to me by Shihan Goody and recognized by Shihan Palumbo. However, I am not Japanese, nor do I have any ties to the any of the modern organizations claiming sovereignty over the Ninja heritage.   Most of these organizations are engulfed in constant political in-fighting about who is legitimate, whose application of skills is more authentic, and who are the true masters.   Although I appreciate the desire to justify their style and position, this arrogant stance has resulted in a constant battle to claim supremacy over something that can never possibly be contained.

I never entered this political arena and I never will. I simply remain diligent on my path to reconstruct a valid system based on the knowledge bestowed upon me combined with personal insights from 30 years of teaching the Kurai Kotori art. Both then and now I believe that this style maintains the essence of what it means to be a Ninja.

Creating my own style has also allowed me a certain freedom. This is the "Art" aspect of martial arts. My journey realized through the creation of a new system based on old information. Japanese in spirit, but 100% American in ingenuity and vision. In all things there must be a beginning.

Now, as I reflect back on that beginning, and the decades that followed, I realize I have trained many generations of black belts and there have been great memories, painful losses, and every level of emotion in-between. But such a journey is one of self-effacement where the good and the bad must be embraced and used to promote growth. More than anything, I am reminded of another wise quote. "If a wealthy man dies hoarding his riches, then he lived poorly." The meaning of this statement is all too clear. All that is not given is lost.

First Kurai Kotori Ninja Training Camp 1986

The book you are about to read is actually an updated version of one of the many training manuals I created for my students during those early years. It was back then that I titled these tomes as the "Arcanum of Ninja Tactics" and they have survived in many incarnations ever since.

This volume, *Legacy of the Shadow Warrior* is the first step to understanding the Kurai Kotori Ninjutsu path. The goal of this book is to put the entire art into perspective so those who choose to study its teachings will have a complete understanding of the skills contained in the system.

Always the Quest — Mark Steven Grove

CHAPTER ONE

HISTORICAL TIES

CHAPTER ONE
HISTORICAL TIES

The Ninja of Japan are certainly among the most celebrated espionage agents the world has ever known. However, the term "Ninja" refers to a myriad of individuals who operated both inside and outside the laws of Japan's Feudal government. These "Ninja" sprang up from all classes of

Ninja Hero

Ninja Mystic

people.   We can only speculate on the motivations and exploits of these warriors because their actual origins are extremely obscure.   There was no single founder of the techniques and philosophies that made up the art that has since become known as "Ninjutsu" (the art of stealth and perseverance).   In fact, much of what is known about the Ninja is often exaggerated as myth and legend.   Depending on the historian, the Ninja was either a hero, a vagabond, a terrorist, a mystic, an assassin or a mercenary.   None of these statements would be entirely incorrect.   In actuality, anyone with sufficient motivation and skill could walk the path of the shadow-warrior.   A Ninja could be anyone, even Buddhist priests were not above adopting the cloak and dagger approach when protecting their temples from unscrupulous marauders. The one point that all historians do agree upon is that the Ninja's dedication to the path of intrigue and deception was unparalleled.

Now it is my turn to act as historian. Throughout all my years of training in the Japanese arts, I have been exposed to a great deal of information. In an attempt to honor the warriors known as Ninja, I will offer an abbreviated history that denotes important events that led to the birth and evolution of the craft of Ninjutsu. Although it is my duty as a historian to "interpret" the past, it is also my duty to look at it from different perspectives, which many times leads to the development of a "reinterpreted" past. This is important because many historians approach subjects with a one sided view. They paint a picture that best suits their position. In many cases, writers of Japanese history approach things from the particularly annoying perspective where Ninja are stereotyped as black-clad villains who assassinate their victims with no conscience or regrets. This is truly sad. It's like saying every cowboy in the American West was a gunfighter with no regard for law and order. It just isn't true. It is important that we realize that each individual ever born on this planet has their own mind. People are not automatons who simply walk around like zombies performing pre-programmed tasks. There is a human factor that cannot be denied. Although it is much easier to view an entire race, class, or culture as being a certain way, it is also ignorant. We must take off the blinders long enough to take a look at all the possibilities, realizing that no matter how much we think we know....we weren't there. That is why I have always attempted to free my students from the static constraints of fact in an effort to bring about a deeper understanding of the Ninja. However, there are indeed certain factors in history that are unarguable. When wars were fought, who lived and who died, and many other things that were chronicled in detail by the historians of the time. Hopefully, these feudal scribes were honest men who attempted to keep an accurate account of events rather than being politically motivated to write things that would make

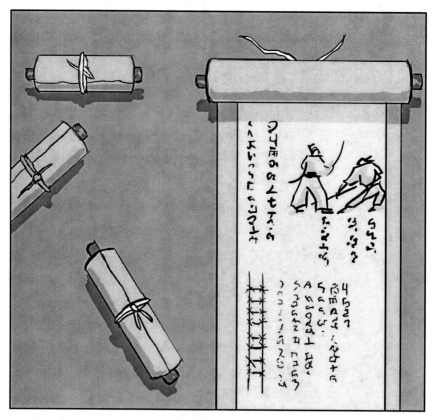

Ninja Scrolls

whoever they served look good in the eyes of following generations. We can only hope this was the case. Although we can gain a great deal from these historical records, what about what wasn't written? We can only speculate on the many deeds that were carried out by the thousands of Ninja that lived throughout Japan's history. The scrolls and books that do exist is where most historians gather what information they can. These cover only a small percentage of what occurred throughout the many generations. Although these documents have proven extremely valuable in helping to build a strong perception of what Ninja did, the reality is the majority of Ninja activities probably went unnoticed, which makes sense. Only the missions that were extremely high profile would be heavily documented because of the large scale effect they had on the country. However, it is very likely, if not obvious, that the Ninja also performed thousands of smaller scale operations that had more subtle effects on those around them. There must have been countless cases where Ninja were responsible for stopping wars before they could start, where simple bits of information were gathered to ensure alliances, where certain undesirables who could have disrupted peace were made to disappear, and where an enemy's weaknesses were uncovered to ensure a quick victory if war was unavoidable. Without these more subtle missions, there are many events in Japan's history that would have been significantly altered. However, my conjecture is irrelevant, we must begin our quest with historical records.

CHINESE INFLUENCE

From the written records that do exist, it is evident that the fundamental ideas that would later evolve into Ninjutsu came from China. This information came from the Chinese text on the Military arts known as "The Art of War," which was written by the great strategy expert Sun Tzu (400-320 B.C.). The detailed knowledge contained in Sun Tzu's writings included information about *tactical maneuvering, the psychology of warfare, choosing objectives wisely, how to mount a proper offensive, the value of surprise, the need for a unified command,* and most important, *maintaining secrecy.* This information was introduced to Japan sometime during the 6th century. For hundreds of years after that point, these strategic skills were developed and refined by a group of mystic shamans known as "Yamabushi," which roughly translates as "One who sleeps in the mountains." These warrior-mystics are considered to be the forerunners of the Ninja. They practiced the arts of Shugendo,

which were comprised of Buddhism, Shinto, Taoism, and Folk lore. These priests also received training in the Chinese martial arts, which, most would agree, served as the basis for the evolution of many of the unarmed combat and weaponry skills that would develop in Japan.

Yamabushi

CREATURES OF LEGEND

It was also during this time that stories of "Karasu tengu," or "Crow goblins" arose. These creatures were said to have the body of a man and the head and wings of a bird. They were supposedly endowed with magical abilities such as teleportation and spell casting. Karasu tengu were considered to be mischievous in their actions, plaguing those who passed through their domain with a variety of

Karasu Tengu

tricks and traps. Karasu tengu were said to be great warriors with a high degree of martial skill, especially in the art of swordsmanship. They communicated with one another through telepathy rather than the spoken word. It was also said that they could possess and speak through humans and were capable of projecting themselves into the dreams of warriors in order to impart special knowledge such as unique fighting techniques or spiritual insights. On rare occasions, they would also transform themselves into human form in order to mingle with other humans. Warriors of great skill were said to have fought and killed a Karasu tengu, but they were shocked when their fallen opponent would magically transform into a wounded crow before their very eyes. Although these stories were more legend than reality, it was a strange coincidence that Yamabushi were also said to possess similar mystical powers that they drew from rituals practiced in mountain sanctuaries. Over time, stories of Yamabushi and Tengu were interwoven. A new breed of Tengu emerged into existence. These were known as

Yamabushi-Tengu

"Yamabushi-tengu," or "Mountain goblins." These Tengu were more human than their predecessors. Yamabushi - tengu were said to be bare-footed elderly men with long noses and white hair. These long nosed human-tengu were usually in charge of bird-tengu. The king of all Tengu was known as Sojobo, who was famous for teaching Minamoto Yoshitsune the secrets of the Kurama Hachi-ryu Yamabushi at the temple on Mount Kurama.

Sojobo teaches Minamoto Yoshitsune

Throughout future periods in Japan, the tales of Tengu flourished, and their connection with those who would later be known as "Ninja," was inevitable. As in all cultures, stories of myth and legend always have some basis in fact. Something that binds the imagination to the real world. In today's age, such things are dismissed as superstition, but in the days of old, the creative power of the mind enabled men to accomplish supernatural feats. Thus, a strong belief in something often makes it real.

SPIRITUAL SHADOW WARRIORS

Starting in the 6th century many Buddhist monks came over from China to set up temples in Japan. Many Japanese saw this as a threat to the already established Shinto religion. Conflict was inevitable. Therefore, the monks maintained a combat system called "Chuan Fa," which stemmed from the arts taught to the Shaolin in

China, however, in Japan, the art became known as "Kempo." Originally the only weapon used by the monks was the staff, but in an effort to preserve their religious beliefs, they also became renowned with the halberd, spear and axe. The priests who practiced these skills became known as

Shaolin Monk

"Sohei," or "Warrior-monks." Over time, due to continued religious upheavals, it became necessary for these monks to develop another system known as "Himitsu Kempo," or "Secret fist of law." This art was created as a means of fighting from the shadows, but not with fists. Instead, the Sohei used information gathering to further their goal of attaining true religious freedom. Although these monks became very skilled at spying, there were many things they could not do because of their religious vows. Because of these limitations, the Sohei turned to those who lived in nearby villages. Many of these people relied on the temples as a source of wisdom and guidance. The Sohei trained many of these commoners

Sohei Warrior

in both the religious and fighting arts. Some of these men and women became known as "Jisamurai," or "Rural warriors," many of whom would become foot soldiers for the warlords of the provinces in which they resided. A select few of these rural warriors were taught the arts of Himitsu Kempo to assist the monks in their clandestine activities. Many of these specially trained warriors were very devout to the religious aspects of training and carried out their espionage duties as a demonstration of their faith. The arts studied by these warriors eventually evolved into "Nimpo," or the "Law of patience." Patience being one of the most prominent virtues in any religion, it was their adherence to this concept that made them so effective. A Nimpo warrior would never act rashly, but would instead rely on information gathering and strategic planning to ensure victory while rarely engaging the enemy in combat. Because of their subversive activities, the Buddhist temples would eventually become one of the most powerful and influential institutions in Japan. Beyond the Nimpo warriors, others sought to use the skills of the Sohei to protect their villages against bandits, repel marauding armies and lead revolts against the unfair taxation imbued upon them by the government. Straying from their religious connections, the methods utilized by these men and women were widely focused on deception, involving skills like surprise attack, poisoning, assassination, forgery and sabotage. The art that would become Ninjutsu was taking shape.

THE FIRST ORGANIZED NINJA GROUPS

The actual origins of the first Ninja seem to stem from two regions located within the Suzuka mountain range where the Yamabushi and Sohei were said to reside. These areas were known as Iga (ee-ga) and Koga (koo-ga). These regions were very close to one another, both culturally and politically. Koga was actually a part of the Omi province and Iga was a region in itself, but in all respects they were considered to be the same area. The Suzuka mountain range was a mysterious place made up of extremely dense terrain that made travel very difficult. Because of this, it became a place of refuge for renegades, traitors and thieves who had no other place to turn.

Iga / Koga Region

During the Heian period (794-1185) many warriors within the Iga and Koga regions sought instruction from the monks in order to increase their efficiency in combat. Those fortunate enough to study from the Yamabushi and Sohei were taught the true value of subterfuge in warfare. It is said that the first established Koga groups came together around the year 940. There were eight original Koga families. They were the Koga, Ugai, Naikii,

Koga Crest

Mochizuki, Akutagawa, Ban, Nagano and Ueno. These eight groups were known as the "Koga Hachi Tengu," or "Eight Tengu of Koga." Although these families began to develop heavily at this time, they were *not* considered to be actual martial traditions (ryu). They were known as "Gumi," or "Groups," who did not follow strict training regimens, but instead learned what they could from wherever they could. This formed the basis for an eclectic approach to training. Eventually the eight original Koga families evolved into 53 separate groups, including, Taro Gumi, Shinpi Gumi, Byaku Gumi, Hiryu Gumi, Sasaki Gumi, Kuruya Gumi, Tatara Gumi, Fukiwara Gumi, Tomo Gumi, Suguwara Gumi, Otomo Gumi, Isshu Gumi, Kawachi Yon Tengu Gumi, Taira Gumi, Kakuryu Gumi and Tachibana Hachi Tengu Gumi.

THE SHADOW ARTS FLOURISH

It was during the Kamakura period (1185-1333) that the Ninja arts prospered. The Iga region formed their own internal government that was ruled by a council, which was good for them because it was widely known that they were resentful of outside authority. Koga also had a limited form of self-government. The Omi region, which Koga was a part of, was ruled by the Rokkaku family. The Rokkaku allowed the Koga the freedom to rule over themselves as long as they were supportive of the Rokkaku families endeavors. Ultimately the ability to govern their own interests gave Iga and Koga Ninja the

Iga Crest

ability to work independently, hiring themselves out to anyone without any restrictions. Many Iga and Koga Ninja actually became vassals to clans outside their own regions, serving them dutifully. This meant that different Iga and Koga Ninja were often times pitted against one another simply because they chose to ally themselves with opposing forces. Although this seems like a breach of loyalties, it was not uncommon for a Ninja, or a group of Ninja, to be dedicated to a specific warlord.

The Kamakura era also saw the emergence of many myths and legends concerning the abilities of the Ninja. These stories arose because of the fact that the Ninja's actions were rarely observed, so the Ninja's enemies could only evaluate their capabilities based on the results. So when whole garrisons of Samurai fell ill, or important personages disappeared without a trace, it was blamed on Ninja magic. None suspected simple poisoning or kidnapping. Instead, the overly superstitious Japanese people began convincing themselves that the Ninja had a wide variety of supernatural powers at their disposal. They believed these powers stemmed from ties to the vicious "Oni" devils and the mischievous "Tengu" crow goblins that were said to be in league with the Ninja because of their alliance with the Yamabushi. Even those who did not fear the Ninja as supernatural entities did not underestimate their prowess as both warriors and information gatherers.

BIRTH OF THE SHOGUN

The Kamakura period also brought about Japan's first Shogun (Military dictator) in the form of Minamoto Yoritomo. Actually, the term "Shogun," which meant "Supreme general," was first used by military leaders in the early 700s when they were campaigning against tribal factions in the northern part of the country. However, the term was not widely used for over 400 years until Minamoto Yoritomo gained military control over the entire country in 1185. Then in 1192 the Emperor

Minamoto Yoritomo

43

officially gave him the title of Shogun. The Shogunate eventually dominated the government, taking over all the judicial, administrative and military functions of the country. The Shogun appointed provincial warlords in an effort to maintain total control. However, the following Minamoto successor, Yoriie, proved unable to do the same. During his reign, the powerful Hojo clan served as Regent to the Shogun. The first Regent, Hojo Tokimasa, was able to seize complete control of the countries laws, revenues

Hojo Crest

and military, which for all intents and purposes, made him the real leader of Japan. The Hojo clan maintained their Regent status until the 7th successor, Hojo Takatoki, who was arrogant and incompetent, attempted to exile the Emperor. The Emperor escaped his grasp and waged war against the Hojo leader. In the end, Takatoki killed himself on July 4th 1333. Unfortunately, despite Takatoki's inept leadership, the Emperor was unable to truly restore imperial rule. In 1338 a new Shogun, Ashikaga Takauji assumed control of the country.

THE WARRING PERIOD

During the Ashikaga Shogunate (1338 -1568), the northern and southern dynasties waged a ruthless war against one another. It was then that Ninja emerged in force. They were put into action to gather intelligence, assassinate important military targets and deliver information to allied

forces. At this point the Ninja were openly accepted, but only because their solid tactics won battles. However, despite their involvement, when the wars ended, the Samurai savored the glory as the Ninja faded back into the shadows.

Ashikaga Crest

The 15th century also saw the plague of civil war. In the year 1467 the battle known as the Onin war started, which for the most part, was over the succession of the Ashikaga Shogunate under the 7th successor, Ashikaga Yoshihisa. This Shogunate paled in comparison to prior governmental rule. Neither the Emperor nor the Shogun himself had the skill or power necessary to control all the feudal factions in Japan. The number of separate ruling families numbered around 260, so in effect, Japan was split up into 260 different countries, each ruled by a powerful independent Daimyo with a large army. With no centralized rule, these Daimyo settled disputes with one another in battle.

It was during this chaotic time that the Rokkaku clan summoned the aid of their Koga allies. The Koga answered the call along with a small contingent of Iga Ninja. Rokkaku Takayori, head of the Rokkaku family, had openly defied the Shogun, Ashikaga Yoshihisa, and had to flee back to his home in the Omi province. The Shogun and his army pursued, setting up camp at Magari village in the Koga region. It was there that the Koga Ninja and their Iga allies struck. The Shogun's forces were formidable, but they were no match for the unorthodox tactics of the Ninja. Shadow warriors attacked with fire arrows in the dead of night, but they did not target the Shogun's Samurai. They used their fiery missiles to ignite the Shogun's provisions, attempting to destroy valuable food, water and medical supplies. During the chaos of the fire attack, another group of Ninja entered and scattered their horses, eliminating the possibility of a strategic retreat. The Ninja kept the army pinned down for

Ninja fire arrow assault

many days. As events unfolded, the Shogun was stricken by disease while in the field, and without proper food, water and medical supplies, he wouldn't last long. The Shogun's men attempted to get him out on foot, but far too many Ninja in the surrounding forest barred their escape. The Shogun eventually died and his army was destroyed. The Koga and Iga Ninja were given high praise. This time became known as the "Sengoku Jidai," or "Age of Civil War" (1467 - 1603). During this time, the Ninja and their specialized skills were in high demand. Ninja were not only used for their spying abilities, they were also involved in many battles that were fought by individual Daimyo in an effort to gain control over Kyoto.

It was also during the Muromachi period that the Portuguese traders brought firelocks to Japan (1543). Although guns were a hindrance to the Samurai, they were a blessing to the Ninja. Through the use of refined black powder, the Ninja were able to create more reliable smoke grenades, explosive arrows, land mines and small hand-held cannons. Ninja were more powerful than ever. The famed general, Tokugawa Ieyasu, employed a small group of Koga Ninja to help him free some of his family members

Tokugawa Crest

that were being held by the Imagawa clan. The Imagawa were holding these hostages to ensure Tokugawa's alliance with them, but once they were freed by the Ninja, Tokugawa joined forces with Oda Nobunaga. Nobunaga is often referred to as one of the three unifiers of Japan, but he was not a pleasant man. Nobunaga was a great military leader obsessed with the thought of ruling the country. His goal was to unite Japan under a single sword (Tenka Fubu), bringing all the warlords of the land together under his leadership...whether they liked it or not.

NOBUNAGA SEIZES CONTROL

Nobunaga's dreams of power soon became a reality when, during the Azuchi-Momoyama period, he drove the 15th Ashikaga successor, Yoshiaki, from office, assumed military control of the country and moved into the capital city of Kyoto. Although Nobunaga was never named Shogun, he was definitely the most powerful man in Japan. Many were displeased. The Sasaki family hired a large force of Ninja from Iga and Koga and combined them with an army of Sasaki Samurai. Sasaki's goal was to kill Oda Nobunaga. Sasaki split his army into three groups. The first group

Oda Nobunaga

was made up of Ninja from the Mikumo Gumi, Takanose Gumi, Mizuhara Gumi and Inui Gumi. The second group was made up of Koga Ninja from many of the 53 families. The third division was made up of Sasaki Samurai. During the battle against Nobunaga, one of Sasaki's Ninja, Mikumo Iyo No Kami, who led one of his forces, betrayed Sasaki and joined Nobunaga. The Sasaki attempt on Nobunaga ultimately failed.

Nobunaga continued his quest to unify the nation. He was an extremely heartless ruler, especially when it came to Buddhists. This was because Nobunaga believed heavily in the Christian faith. Then in the year 1571 Nobunaga did the unimaginable. He massacred over 100,000 men, women and children in an attack against the Buddhist temples on Mount Hiei and the surrounding region. He did this because since early in Japan's history, the warrior-monks of

Nobunaga destroys the Monastery

Mount Hiei were heavily involved in both the political and military dealings of the country. Seeing this as a threat to his position, Nobunaga destroyed the monastery and all those with any ties to it. It was because of this incident that many Ninja took on the personal task of disposing of such a tyrant. One such Ninja, Sugitani Zenjubo, who was a very skilled warrior from Koga, came very close to succeeding, but not close enough. Nobunaga continued to wreak havoc throughout Japan. During his campaign, he eventually took possession of the Omi province, which also included the Koga region. A lord from Koga known as Takigawa, tried to convince Nobunaga to decimate the Koga families that ruled the province. Takigawa made this suggestion in the hopes that he would be named head of the Omi province after the other families were routed. Tokugawa Ieyasu convinced Nobunaga that such an act was unwarranted. The Koga were left alone....for the time being.

Years later, during the battle of Iga, known as "Tensho Iga No Ran" (1581), Nobunaga sent his son, Katsuyori, along with a vast army of Samurai to rid the land of the defiant men and women of Iga. Nobunaga understood the power of guerilla tactics. He knew the Ninja would never submit to his authority, and would therefore have to be destroyed. Although Katsuyori's Samurai were well trained, they were no match for the cunning Ninja of Iga. Through numerous surprise attacks, Katsuyori's troops suffered extreme losses. It was not long after the battle began that Katsuyori and his surviving Samurai retreated in disgrace.

Tensho Iga No Ran

Nobunaga was infuriated by his sons defeat, he devised an in-depth plan and began gathering an army. Nobunaga himself led an army of 46,000 Samurai against the 4,000 Ninja that inhabited Iga. Hearing about the imminent battle, many of the Ninja from Koga traveled to Iga to assist their brothers in defending their domain. The battle

lasted a little under a week. Even though the warriors of Iga and Koga put up a good fight, they were no match for the superior forces of Nobunaga. The Ninja fled in all directions.

Ninja flee their mountain villages

Those who successfully escaped the region sought employment with many of the lords who they served in the past. Most were accepted as permanent members of these clans from that point on. For their involvement in the battle, Nobunaga ordered the deaths of many of the Koga Ninja and had their villages in Omi destroyed.

Then in 1582, Oda Nobunaga was assassinated by Mitsuhide Akechi, who was once one of Nobunaga's trusted Samurai and perhaps secretly a Ninja. Although considered an assassination, Mitsuhide somehow forced Nobunaga to commit seppuku (ritual suicide). Records show that Mitsuhide was killed 13 days later at the "Incident at Honnoji," but it was rumored in whispers among Ninja that he started a new life as a priest under the name "Tenkai."

Nobunaga forced to commit Seppuku

Nobunaga's two most skilled Generals, Toyotomi Hideyoshi and Tokugawa Ieyasu remained in control, but were also targets for assassination. Once again, war broke out to determine who would become the next leader of the country. Tokugawa, who was out in battle at the time of Nobunaga's death wished to return to his headquarters in Okazaki, but with his life in danger he knew he would need a powerful escort. Tokugawa resorted to asking the Ninja leader Hanzo Hattori to serve as his protector for the length of the journey. Hanzo was perhaps the most famous Ninja in Japanese history. Hanzo was actually a Samurai who

Hanzo Hattori

made the transition to Ninja. He was a vassal of the Tokugawa family who was trained in all aspects of combat, but became known as the "Great lancer" due to his exceptional skill with the spear.

Hanzo's first major battle was in 1557 at the age of 16 when Tokugawa Ieyasu attacked Uzichijo. His prowess in combat was remarkable. Two of his most famous battles took place in Kanagawa in 1570 and Mikatagahara in 1572, in which he proved his Ninja skills were as powerful as his battlefield exploits, making him one of Tokugawa's most prized shadow warriors. Hattori accepted the offer and, along with the Koga Ninja *Taro Shiro*, began assembling as many Iga Ninja as he could find to become Tokugawa's private bodyguards. On the trek to Okazaki, they faced many perils, but in the end, Tokugawa was delivered safely to his headquarters. Ieyasu rewarded Hanzo by giving him control of over 300 renegade Ninja from Iga and Koga, all of which became permanent vassals of Tokugawa. Hanzo served the Tokugawa family loyally until his death in 1596 at the hands of Fuma Kotaro, a Ninja pirate.

TOYOTOMI ASSUMES POWER

The war ended in 1590 and Toyotomi Hideyoshi assumed power over the country. Whereas Nobunaga attempted to unify the country through the use of force, Toyotomi instead focused on the subtleties of an organized administration. His national structure consisted of regional warlords who were allowed to remain independent, as long as they cooperated peacefully with one another. This allowed Toyotomi to follow his true ambition. Toyotomi wanted to expand the Japanese empire over all of Asia. In 1592 and again in 1597, he invaded Korea. He was successful in seizing a sizeable portion of the land. Because of his successful campaigns Toyotomi began amassing enormous wealth which he spread throughout the Imperial court and on to

Toyotomi Crest

the various lords throughout Japan. This made him extremely popular. However, Toyotomi's overall objective was to use his position in Korea as a launching point for the conquest of China. Unfortunately this dream was never realized. In the year 1598 Toyotomi died, leaving his title, his lands and his wealth to his young son, Hideyori. Not yet old enough to effectively run the country, it was decided that Tokugawa would step in until Hideyori came of age. However, Tokugawa had no intention of returning power to the young lord, and instead began plotting to take control of the country himself.

TOKUGAWA SHOGUNATE

During the battle of Sekigahara (1600) the Ninja re-emerged in force. Toyotomi Hideyori finally came of age and was ready to assume his role as leader of Japan. Tokugawa refused to step down. Once again, all the warlords of the country split into two groups, those loyal to the Toyotomi name, and those loyal to Tokugawa. After 3 years and many battles, Tokugawa's army and his secret Ninja force finally routed Toyotomi's forces, and the Emperor officially named Tokugawa as Shogun because he provided documentation, which although questionable, established him as a descendant of the Minamoto family. However, despite his illustrious lineage, many warlords remained dedicated to restoring the Toyotomi name to its rightful place.

SANADA UPRISING

The Sanada family, a renowned Samurai clan that had been banished from their province because they would not side with Tokugawa, regrouped in the mountains, secretly plotting against the Tokugawa Shogunate. They remained hidden for many years until they were forced to re-emerge

Sanada Crest

prematurely when one of Tokugawa's Koga Ninja assassinated the head of the Sanada family, leaving his son Sanada Yukimura as clan leader. Yukimura discovered that Tokugawa planned to lay siege to Osaka castle to eliminate Hideyori Toyotomi once and for all, ending any hopes the Toyotomi clan had of regaining the Shogunate. Although the Toyotomi clan had a vast army, most of them were Ronin (masterless samurai) who worked solely for profit, which made them difficult to rely upon. Realizing that something had to be done, Sanada Yukimura renounced his Samurai status and gathered a small band of renegade Ninja to aid the Toyotomi clan in defending Osaka castle. Legend says these Ninja were known as the "Sanada Ten Braves" and the group consisted of Kirigakure Saizo, Sarutobi Sasuke, Miyoshi Isa, Miyoshi Seikai, Anayama Kosuke, Kakei Juzo, Unno Rokuro, Yuri Kamanosuke, Nezu Jinpachi, and Mochizuki Rokuro.

WINTER SIEGE OF OSAKA CASTLE

Sanada and his Ninja were highly successful during what was referred to as the *Winter Campaign at Osaka* (November 1614 to January 1615). Sanada helped fortify Osaka castle with a barbican that extended over the castle's

Winter Siege

southwest corner that housed hundreds of slots for firearms and special gates that opened to drop heavy logs and stones on enemies as they attempted to storm the castle. With 7,000 men under his command, Sanada repeatedly defeated Tokugawa forces. To increase their advantage, Sanada dispatched one of his Ninja to infiltrate the Tokugawa camp to distribute a hallucinogenic drug into their food and water supplies. Although Tokugawa forces were far greater, they could not penetrate the castles defenses. But just as Tokugawa's forces could not get in, Toyotomi forces could not get out. Ieyasu proposed a peaceful resolution with Toyotomi that would put an end to the attacks, but Toyotomi must agree that the outer moat of the castle would be destroyed. Toyotomi agreed, but when Tokugawa's forces gained entrance to the castle, they destroyed the inner moat as well. If Toyotomi opposed Tokugawa again, the castle would not be able to withstand an assault.

SUMMER SIEGE OF OSAKA CASTLE

In April 1616, Tokugawa's Ninja reported that Toyotomi was gathering forces to rebuild the moat at Osaka castle. The final battle took place south of Osaka castle at Tennoji, where Toyotomi Ninja and Samurai fought side by side against Tokugawa's forces. However, Tokugawa's army proved too strong and Toyotomi's forces retreated back to Osaka castle. Tokugawa brought in several large cannon and began firing upon the castle from a distance. Unable to effectively defend against the superior weapons, the castle erupted into flames. Fleeing the castle, the last of

Summer Seige

Toyotomi's forces were defeated by Tokugawa's troops. The young Hideyori Toyotomi committed ritual suicide as the castle fell around him. Tokugawa finally won.

TOKUGAWA REIGN SOLIDIFIED

In 1616, the title of Shogun was past on to Tokugawa Ieyasu's third son, Hidetada. Actually, Hidetada was officially named Shogun in 1605, but his elderly father maintained authority until his death at the age of 75. It was during this time that Tokugawa Hidetada made the initial steps to halt the majority of foreign trade, believing that outside influence was a detriment to the country's prosperity.

Hidetada Tokugawa

Hidetada was also effective at banishing Christianity from the country in an effort to restore Japan's inherent religions to their former glory. Hidetada married Oeyo Oda and they had two sons, Iemitsu and Tadanaga.

NINJA RETURN HOME

Many of the Ninja that fled during the battle of Tensho Iga no Ran, returned to their former home in dark mountain forests of the Iga province to become farmers, or at least pose as farmers. The leaders of the province organized them into small elite units that were expected to serve the government loyally. As compensation for their obedience, they were allowed to keep a small portion of what their farms produced. However, although they were considered a part of the military, they did not receive a stipend as Samurai did. For all practical purposes, they were no longer the rebellious heroes of the land. They were reduced to commoners who were sometimes called to serve as intelligence gatherers.

Return to the Mountains

ISOLATING JAPAN

Tokugawa Iemitsu was named as inheritor to the Shogun title in 1623 when his father retired. However, Hidetada, like his father, remained in power and continued his reign. He was responsible for strengthening the Shogunate by reducing what little influence the Emperor had on the country even further. He successfully closed Japan's borders with the exception of Dejima, which had a small Dutch trading post and Nagasaki, which was still open to Chinese ships. Beyond that, all other trade with other countries was cut off. In 1632 Hidetada died and Iemitsu officially became shogun. During Iemitsu's first years in power, the clans that still opposed the Shogun were moved to the areas of Choshu and Satsuma, which were located to the far south of Japan. This distance caused those in Choshu and Satsuma great economic strife. This was because of the Tokugawa policy that every Daimyo in the land would spend half their time in the capital of Edo. Tokugawa made family members of each Daimyo remain as permanent residents of Edo to ensure their continued loyalty. For those Daimyo with provinces close to Edo, the travel costs were minimal, but for those who didn't, had a high financial burden, causing those in the Choshu and Satsuma to gain a distinct dislike for the Tokugawa regime.

THE LAST CHRISTIAN REVOLT

It wasn't until 1638, at a battle known as the battle at "Shimabara," that the Ninja were used for anything of renowned importance. Within Shimabara castle, several hundred peasants and Christians were revolting. This battle was over religious beliefs. Tokugawa Hidetada had begun a vicious persecution of anything Christian in the 1620's and Tokugawa Iemitsu continued into the 1630's, and he wanted those who sought to resurrect it destroyed. A small group of Ninja were dispatched to help end the revolt. This team was made up of Mochizuki Heidayu, Akutagawa Kiyouemon, Tomei Gohei, Mochizuki Yoemon, Kamogai Kanuemon, Akutagawa Shichirobei, Natsumi Kakuno-suke, Yamanaka Jutayu and Iwane Kanbei. They arrived at Shimabara on January 4th. Within days, they successfully created a map, stole food and water supplies and infiltrated the castle disguised as guards, all of which led to the fall of the castle on January 24th.

Christian Revolt

NEW HEROES AND VILLAINS

The Koga and Iga Ninja who remained at the capital were soon promoted. Some where assigned to an elite gun corps, others became personal guards, and some even joined the local police force. Some of the most prominent Ninja and Samurai became "Hatamoto," or "Direct vassals to the Shogun." These positions were fleeting. In all respects, they were unemployed, forcing many of them to become "Ronin," or "Masterless warriors." Many became known as "Kabuki-mono," which meant "Crazy ones." These eccentric Ninja and Samurai took on colorful names, wore strange clothing, and took pleasure in terrorizing any

Kabuki Mono

who crossed their path. They were extremely loyal to one another, and in time, the Kabuki-mono numbered over 500,000, many of whom wandered throughout Japan looting towns and villages. However, to every coin there are two sides. Another group emerged simultaneously. These people were called "Machi-yakko," or "Servants of the town," and they consisted of merchants, laborers, fishermen, renegade Ninja and Ronin who had become professional gamblers as a means of earning a living. Everyone in this group took up arms against the Kabuki-mono, serving as protectors against their tyranny. The Machi-yakko became heroes, praised by town and villages across the country for their bravery.

ELITE NINJA

In 1716 Tokugawa Yoshimune was named Shogun. When he assumed the title, he brought in many of his own people to run the government. Among those in his employ were Kishu-Ryu Ninja who were descendants of the Ninja who fled to the Kii province after the battle of Iga 135 years earlier. The Shogun organized the Kishu Ninja into a group called "Oniwaban," which was to be a large scale intelligence unit that would serve as the country's internal security network. The agents in this network were called "Metsuke," which literally meant "Eyes." This new breed of Ninja was no longer restricted to the shadows. Their positions were very high profile and respectable. The Shogun assigned a Metsuke to serve a Daimyo in every province in the land. These agents were very polite, diplomatic and

Metsuke

most importantly, attentive to the events of the province. This made it very difficult for any Daimyo to plot against the Shogun without the risk of being discovered. In essence, the Metsuke, because of their elite status, could openly map all the details of a castle in full view of everyone, noting its strengths and weaknesses. They could keep track of the number of Samurai employed by the daimyo, and they could investigate any issue that seemed suspicious to them. This information would then be sent directly to the Shogun reference.

A SECRET UNDERWORLD

By the late 1700's the Machi-yakko (servants of the town) had evolved into a group known as *Yakuza*. This word, which roughly translated means "worthless" comes from a card game called "Hanafuda," or "Flower cards." The goal of the game is to gather three cards that total 19 or under. Anything over 19 is a losing hand. The word YA meant 8, KU meant 9 and ZA meant three. This hand would total 20, which is a worthless hand, thus the name signifies someone who is an outsider of society. This group was mostly made up of the poor, landless misfits of society, which was perfect for many renegade Ninja and Ronin who could use their skills to attain high positions of power within the Yakuza hierarchy.

Yakuza

YAKUZA HIERARCHY

The Yakuza families were based on a *Father* (oyabun) *Child* (kobun) relationship. The leader of a Yakuza family was

considered to be the parent to all those in his group. Initiation into a Yakuza family was a very ornate ritual. Unlike a classical martial tradition which required an oath written on a scroll in the applicants

Yakuza Bow

own blood and then burned at an alter, the Yakuza simply exchanged sake (rice wine) cups, filled to a level consistent with their rank, to symbolize their Oyabun-Kobun relationship. This act was performed before a Shinto alter, which gave it religious significance. The Kobun position, although always subservient to the Oyabun, consisted of many levels. These levels included; under-boss, officers, enlisted and apprentices. This structure was not unlike the hierarchy used by the Ninja families of Iga and Koga.

JAPAN OPENS ITS GATES

In 1853, Commodore Matthew Calbraith Perry sailed into Edo harbor to open up trade with Japan. Many Japanese were amazed at western technology, the most prominent being a miniature locomotive. Many were eager to embrace western influence, others saw it as a great evil that sought to undermine Japan's traditional values. It was at this time that the Iga Ninja Sawamura Jinsaburo Yasusuke was dispatched to gather information on these "Invaders."

Commodore Perry

What he discovered was that the western colonial fleets were extremely powerful and it was obvious they were intent on instilling their views on the Japanese. The initial response was decidedly anti-western. Especially in Satsuma and Choshu, two regions who already had issues with the Shogunate. The Samurai of Satsuma and Choshu, who were called "Shi Shi," or "Men of high purpose" were angry that the Shogun had signed an agreement with the western barbarians without the consent of the Emperor. They viewed the Emperor as a god, thus creating a slogan "Revere the Emperor, expel the Barbarians," which spread quickly across Japan. The Samurai and Ninja of Satsuma and Choshu along with others who had the same views about western influence armed themselves. They would not let foreigners invade their country without a fight. From that point forward many terrorist-style attacks were carried out, eliminating some of Japan's most prominent leaders. The Shi Shi even attacked western ships, which resulted in an immediate counter-attack. The western ships destroyed both the capitals of Satsuma and Choshu with heavy cannon fire. All that remained were smoking ruins. Tokugawa Yoshinobu became the last of Japan's Shoguns in 1866. By this time, Japan had completely opened itself up to the outside world. The country was now flooded with Dutch, French, British and Russian foreigners. This created a myriad of internal conflicts that weakened the Shogunate and led many to believe is was time to restore power to the Emperor.

RESTORING IMPERIAL RULE

The Meiji period (1868 - 1912) was known as the "Restoration era" because in November of 1867, Shogun Tokugawa Yoshinobu agreed, at least in principle, to step down and return power to the Imperial government. But it was not until after an attack on the imperial palace by the

Emperor Meiji

General Saigo Takamori, who led the Satsuma, Choshu and Tosa clans against the Shogun's army. On January 3rd 1868 the land was reclaimed under the young 16 year old Emperor Mutsuhito, who was renamed "Meiji," which meant "Enlightened rule."

There was quite a bit of unrest but most Daimyo remained neutral, resulting in a minor civil war that ended in 1869. The Emperor was relocated from Kyoto to Edo, which was at that time renamed "Tokyo," or the "Eastern capitol." In order to bring stability to the government, all Daimyo were ordered to relinquish their lands to the Emperor. By 1871 these lands were broken into prefectures and the former Daimyo became members of a newly restructured nobility.

Unlike his father, Emperor Meiji was an advocate of modernization. Thus, a new mass education system was introduced and a plan for a more modern military was taking shape. Western specialists were brought in to create

Foreign Military Experts

railways and develop new industries. Foreign military experts were consulted in an effort to create a more powerful army and naval fleet and overseas expansion was in its initial planning.

DISARMING THE SAMURAI

Seeing no more need for armed Samurai, the Emperor took away the Samurai's right to carry swords. This led to a fierce rebellion. The Samurai had lived a life of privilege for hundreds of years, to take away their status and label them as an unproductive class was asking for trouble. General Saigo, who was responsible for returning power to the Emperor, was against eliminating the Samurai class. Although he had enormous power, the Meiji government did not agree. Saigo had no choice but to declare war on the very government he helped to create. Becoming known as the "Satsuma rebellion of 1877," Saigo Takamori led his Samurai against Kumamoto castle. The Meiji forces, in the form of newly drafted soldiers stood in defense. It was a clash between the old and the new. However, the sword-wielding Samurai and Ninja were no match for the modern Meiji army, who had been trained in western strategy and the use of western weapons. With his original forces of 40,000 Samurai reduced to only a few hundred men, Saigo retreated to his home in Kagoshima where he committed ritual suicide. He lived and died a Samurai. Saigo's death was also the death of the Samurai class, at least in physical form. The spirit would live on. The Meiji restoration was unstoppable. It was made clear that with the Samurai gone, the entire country would live as equals under the rule of the Emperor.

Hanging up the Sword

NEW ARTS FOR A NEW AGE

In the years that followed the Meiji restoration, Japan evolved from an agricultural nation to an industrial nation by assimilating western technology. Because of this change in structure and power, many former Samurai turned their attention from Bujutsu (military arts) to Budo (self-perfection arts). Other arts like Judo (founded by Jigoro Kano in 1882), Kendo (established in 1912), Aikido (founded by Morihei Ueshiba 1925) and Shotokan Karate (founded by Gichin Funakoshi in 1936) would set the standard for modern martial training.

The Evolution of Martial Arts

NINJUTSU TRADITIONS

Based on this brief historical journey we know many things. We know the Ninja operated both outside the law and for the government. We know the Ninja fought both on the battlefield and concealed in the shadows. We know Ninja developed a unique array of weaponry and tools and used unorthodox fighting tactics. We know that Ninja could be both honorable and deceptive. But did these Ninja actually belong to *organized* traditions, or is the art of Ninjutsu as we know it among the newly founded post Meiji arts? From what is known about the Ninja it is difficult, if not nearly impossible, to trace a lineage. Although many claim a direct lineage to various clans, the actual documentation provided by these people is questionable to say the least. Most Japanese scholars agree that Ninjutsu was formalized within the last 100 years and was *never* based on a continuous transmission of information like that found in a traditional Ryu. As a point in fact, it has been said that the *Nihon Kobudo Shinkokai* and *Nihon Kobudo Kyokai*, the two oldest classical arts organizations in Japan have only acknowledged two Ryu as containing traceable Ninjutsu heritage. These are the *Katori Shinto Ryu* (founded mid to late 1400's) and the *Tatsumi-ryu Hyoho* (founded early 1500's). However, even these traditions consider the skills to be auxiliary training that is secondary to their normal training curriculum. No other Ninjutsu organization that exists today are recognized as classical arts. Although many would argue this point, none of them can or are willing to provide scrolls verifying the heritage of their clan predate the Meiji

Katori Shinto Ryu

restoration of 1868, which puts them under the banner of "Modern" arts. This fact clashes with many of the claims of so-called traditional Ninja schools who boast of being up to and above 30th generation systems. The before mentioned *Katori Shinto Ryu* is in its 20th generation and it is considered to be one of the oldest classical schools in Japan dating back to the late 15th century. It was during this time that the Samurai families of Japan began developing, chronicling and maintaining their combative traditions. Before then, it was highly improbable that any formal traditions existed. So, if one claims to belong to a clan that goes beyond 30 generations, that would date them back to the 9th or 10th century, which any reputable historian would agree would be a long, and virtually impossible, time to maintain an un-broken lineage. But is it truly impossible? I've learned that in the world of Ninjutsu, nothing is impossible.

Even though organizations like the *Nihon Kobudo Shinko-kai* do indeed verify scrolls to establish lineage, there are many traditions that do not feel that they need to be verified or recognized by a modern organization in order to validate their system. When you think about it, we are talking about a variety of families who may have been enemies during the feudal era. Turning over their scrolls may indeed prove lineage, but it also would reveal the families innermost secrets. Some traditions may have also had a connection to organized crime which may be looked upon as a stain on their family name. Thus it is understandable why many traditions refused to submit documentation to prove their legitimacy. So it is very possible that many traditions have survived regardless of public recognition.

HISTORICAL WRITINGS

For arguments sake lets say it's true, and the Ninja arts were not passed from master to disciple and chronicled in every detail, what are we studying today? Based on the historical artifacts and writings that do exist, most notably the *Ninpiden* (written by Hattori Hanzo 1653), the *Bansenshukai* (written by Fujibayashi Tasutake in 1676), and the *Shoninki* (written by Natori Masazumi in 1682), it is fairly easy to piece together the many skills that could make up a complex art such as Ninjutsu. All of these writings contain what most would perceive as general references to actual skills, but within them one can find the foundation for the Ninja way of thinking. So although they don't contain detailed fighting methods, they do provide insight into motivation and strategic approach.

Beyond these widely referenced scrolls, there are many fragmented documents that depict that Ninja families maintained specific non-combative skills such as spying or poison making and never actually engaged in any type of physical conflict. Other scrolls show various weapons that would indicate that they were most likely involved in battlefield warfare. It goes to show that the arts maintained by each individual family would most likely be influenced by the region in which they lived, the resources available to them, and their station in society. In the end, there were very few Ninja families that practiced ALL the arts that have come to be collectively known as Ninjutsu.

NINJUTSU TODAY

Practitioners today are exposed to many versions of the Ninja. There are both classical and modernized versions of the art being practiced throughout the world. Not unlike the Iga and Koga families of Feudal Japan, there are large Ninja organizations that have thousands of members and there are some groups that maintain fewer than a hundred. Whether large or small, classic or modern, all of these incarnations of the Ninja path have merit and none of them have exclusive rights to the concept. The reality is, no matter how much one would like to monopolize the art, it is impossible. The answer is simple, *Ninjutsu* is an idea. We must never lose sight of the fact that this was an art that was famous for being unpredictable, adaptable, and most importantly, secretive. The art is completely open to interpretation, and each interpretation is in itself a form of Ninjutsu.

CHAPTER TWO

THE KURAI KOTORI
TRADITION

CHAPTER TWO
THE KURAI KOTORI TRADITION

The Kurai Kotori tradition strives to maintain very realistic skills that are applicable in today's society while also holding firm to the traditional concepts of our Japanese forerunners. The shadow-warriors of old knew that the secret to effective technique could be found in the application of unorthodox tactics. This is perhaps the most important lesson one can learn on their journey towards combative enlightenment.

FAMILY CREST

The Kurai Kotori crest is in the form of a crow with its wings spread out against a night sky. The bird represents the warrior remaining aloft in the sky beyond the reach of their enemies, staying hidden in a cloak of darkness ready to act whenever needed. The Kanji character "Nin," which is housed in the moon translates as the "Sword over the heart," and its meaning is very specific. It dictates that the warrior must remain strong during moments of hardship and that they must respond with perseverance and strength in the face of danger.

Kurai Kotori Crest

79

KURAI KOTORI CLAN HIERARCHY

It is important to have a firm understanding of the hierarchy maintained by the clan. The inner workings of the Kurai Kotori clan must be disciplined if it is to function properly. This is why it is necessary for even the newest member of the clan to become fully aware of the etiquette (reishiki) maintained by its members. Understanding the positions of power within the clan is imperative if one is to learn the value of organization.

JONIN

The leader of the clan is known as the JONIN. This is the Ninja whose mastery of Ninjutsu combined with solid leadership skills, has dedicated themselves to preserving the Kurai Kotori heritage by passing their knowledge on to

Jonin

new generations. The Jonin must be a veteran Ninja who is not just a master of the skills maintained by the clan, but also continues ever forward in search of deeper knowledge in all things. It is the Jonin's insight that guides the clan in all its objectives.

JIKI DESHI

By the Jonin's side are the warriors who have suppressed self in order to become a direct disciple or JIKI DESHI to his teachings. The Jiki Deshi's sole purpose in existence is to benefit their chosen master in every possible way. Such service enables these warriors to receive privileged information direct from the source. The Jiki Deshi endeavor to bring honor to the clan by becoming heir to their Master's name and continuing the tradition upon the Jonin's death or departure. Although this path is tempting

Jiki Deshi

to undertake because of its obvious benefits, it is a path wrought with suffering. Only the most devout warriors are capable of surviving this path for any length of time.

CHUNIN

Directly under the Jonin and his chosen disciples are the clan's sub-commanders. These warriors are considered to be the retainers of the clan, practitioners that are of accomplished rank that become leaders in their own right. The sub-commanders serve as the instructors for those below their rank while doubling as an elite fighting force if needed for a special assignment. The sub-commander is a special breed of warrior who is responsible for the initiates

Chunin - Sub Commanders

within the clan. The sub-commander is referred to as the CHUNIN, and their duties include; overseeing the training of students, keeping morale high within the ranks and defeating internal problems as they occur, if not before.

Genin - Field Agents

GENIN

Directly below the sub-commander are the actual field operatives who carry out the clan's objectives. Ninja operatives are known as GENIN. The field operatives make up the majority of the clan and their skill levels can range anywhere from a new recruit to a seasoned veteran. The role of the Genin within the clan is essential. Their primary duty is to refine their skills on all levels so they are prepared to face any challenge given to them. Many

Genin also specialize is certain aspects of the art. Some may be more adept at stealth and concealment whereas others have superior knowledge of skills such as poison making, reconnaissance, or battlefield tactics.

THE DOJO

The Dojo (training hall) is the place where all warriors congregate to develop their skills through the theory, practice and application of the arts maintained by the Kurai Kotori Ryu. The Dojo is a spiritual location that offers the warrior refuge from the perils of daily existence. Once inside its protective walls, the warrior is shielded from all exterior chaos. The serenity of the Dojo manifests within

The Dojo

the warrior who studies within its confines. Such tranquillity allows for the uninhibited development of body, mind and spirit.

Like a hall of heroes, the Dojo draws its power from those who reside within. Thus the strength and skill possessed by the clan's most accomplished warriors sets the standard for the Dojo's level of energy. These advanced practitioners of the art serve as an inspiration to lower ranking students by providing them with guidance during their training. This is an important factor of the Dojo atmosphere. It is a place where seasoned warriors openly share all of their experiences with those who are new to the path.

Hall of Heroes

DOJO UNIFORM

The training uniform worn by students is a heavy duty single weave black uniform that is extremely durable, which is necessary to accommodate extensive grappling and throwing. The uniform is equipped with a pocket on the inside flap of the lower jacket and the pant cuff is bloused with leg ties. The sleeves of the uniform are tailored to be just below the elbow and the left lapel of the jacket is adorned with the Kurai Kotori crest.

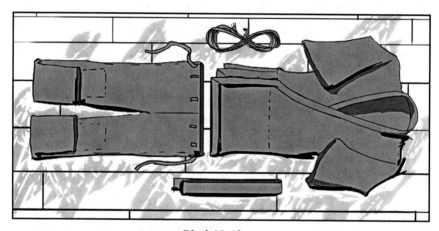

Black Uniform

Leg ties

Family crest

MOUNTAIN SANCTUARY

Whenever possible, the warriors of the Kurai Kotori clan are trained in a wooded or mountainous environment that resembles the concealed training facilities utilized by their ancient forerunners. While hidden deep within these natural surroundings the Kurai Kotori Ninja are exposed to the secrets that cannot be taught as effectively in the training hall. Skills such as: stealth, reconnaissance, infiltration, battlefield formations, trap deployment and survival training. These are the skills that are the subject of study while submerged in Nature's Dojo. This aspect of Ninja training is based on *experience* as opposed to the training which takes place in the Dojo which is based on *repetition*. Only by experiencing the feeling of being pursued by countless shadows or being the warrior responsible for stealthily infiltrating an enemy's camp can one come to understand the skill required to perform such tasks.

Mountain Sanctuary

CLASSICAL GARB

Discarding the training uniform that is used in the Dojo, the warriors of the Kurai Kotori clan don the more appropriate classical garb of the Ninja and begin exploring the shadows. The rank belt is replaced with a long thick sash (obi), split toe shoes (tabi) are worn to maximize sensitivity and stealth, a shroud (zukin) is worn to conceal identity and camouflage human form, and a cloak (gaito) is sometimes used for warmth and shelter.

Classical Garb

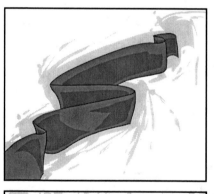

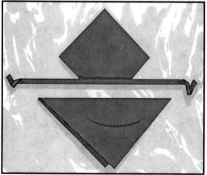

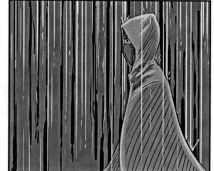

Sash, Split toe shoes, Shroud, and Cloak

TRAINING STRUCTURE

The training structure within the Kurai Kotori Clan has three distinct stages. These three stages are known as the *Shoden* (beginning stage), the *Chuden* (advanced stage) and the *Hiden* (secret stage). Within these three stages there are many levels of training that the student is exposed to. It is by passing the physical and mental tests maintained by each of these levels that the student acquires the knowledge and skill necessary to progress in their training. Not contained within these three stages is the *Okuden* (verbal transmission) aspect of the art. These are insightful lessons on subjects both within and outside the set training regimen.

RANKING AND TITLES

Although rank belts were not used in classical Japanese systems, they do serve a relevant purpose in signifying a student's level on the path. However, instead of a multi-colored belt system, the Kurai Kotori clan has adopted a unique belt rank in which each student is given a black belt upon joining the school. This belt will stay with the student throughout their training, the only thing changing being a small colored stripe on one tip of the belt to signify their level. As their rank increases the previous colored stripe is removed and replaced with a different color to show advancement. Each rank is associated with a title that further signifies a practitioners level on the path.

LEVEL	TITLE	TRANSLATION	RANK
SHODEN	Shoshinsha	Initiate	Black Belt 1 White Stripe
SHODEN	Chi Gakusei	Earth Student	Black Belt 1 Red Stripe
SHODEN	Sui Gakusei	Water Student	Black Belt 1 Orange Stripe
SHODEN	Ka Gakusei	Fire Student	Black Belt 1 Yellow Stripe
SHODEN	Fu Gakusei	Wind Student	Black Belt 1 Green Stripe
CHUDEN	Ku Yushi	Celestial Warrior	Black Belt 1 Blue Stripe
CHUDEN	Tashi	Ninja Master	Black Belt 2 Blue Stripes
CHUDEN	Renshi	Refined Master	Black Belt 3 Blue Stripes
HIDEN	Shinobi	Ninja	Black Belt 4 Blue Stripes
HIDEN	Shinobi Shujin	Ninja Master	Black Belt 5 Blue Stripes
HIDEN	Shinobi Meijin	Ninja Lord	Black Belt 6 Blue Stripes
OKUDEN	Seishin Shugisha	Ninja Spiritualist	Black Belt Blue Border
OKUDEN	Tetsujin	Ninja Philosopher	Black Belt Silver Border
OKUDEN	Kenja	Ninja Sage	Black Belt Gold Border

PRIMARY ARTS & SUB-ARTS

The Kurai Kotori Tradition is a huge system that has over **30 Primary Arts** that house more than **150 Sub-Arts**, making it the most in-depth style in the world. The system in its entirety could be a lifelong journey filled with insights that are unique for every practitioner. Each person on the path excels in different areas and they ultimately form a specialized art that conforms to their natural abilities and interests to create a one of a kind warrior.

PARTIAL LIST OF SKILLS

The following is a visual representation of a few of the skills that make up the multifaceted art of the Ninja.

ACROBATICS

Ninja are taught to maximize their body mobility skills through the use of many specialized drills and techniques. Taiso (calisthenics), Tai Sabaki (movement), Hakari (balance) Ukemi (breakfalls), Kaiten (rolls), Tobi (leaps), Tetobidasu (handsprings), and Kuki Kaiten (aerial flips) are studied in an effort to enhance speed and agility to a refined state. These skills can then be utilized as additives to both armed and unarmed combat by implementing maneuvers during attack and defense as wells as being valuable in climbing, stealth, and concealment.

UNARMED COMBAT

Kurai Kotori Taijutsu (body art) is based on the five elemental furies of earth, water, fire, wind, and celestial. From the four primary elements, the Ninja learns to employ fighting techniques that utilize strength (earth), cunning (water), ferocity (fire), and dexterity (wind). By developing these four attributes equally, the Ninja gains the ability to adapt to situations by allowing the most effective element to emerge when needed (celestial). The unarmed fighting system itself maintains in-depth knowledge of vital targets (genkotsu), muscle attacks (koshiwaza), bone attacks (koppowaza), joint manipulation (kansetsuwaza), throws (nagewaza), pressure attacks (gatamewaza), finger locks (yubiwaza), constriction attacks (shimewaza) escapes and reversals (nukewaza) and defense versus weapons (muto).

SWORDSMANSHIP

Sword skills are the foundation of weaponry training for a Ninja. Training with the Ninja sword (Shinobigatana) cultivates hand/eye coordination and enhances the Ninja's intuition pertaining to the crucial art of timing and combative distancing. The Ninja sword is designed to be utilitarian, stressing usefulness over ornamentation. A shorter blade for speed and concealment combined with a longer hilt for increased leverage and a larger square hand-guard for enhanced protection. Aside from its obvious cutting and striking skills, a Ninja sword has many hidden abilities that enhance its effectiveness. A sturdy scabbard provides a secondary weapon, a container of blinding powder can be expelled into an opponents eyes, and a long length of cord can be used to entangle or flail the scabbard.

FOUR BASIC WEAPONS

There are four basic weapons that serve as a solid foundation for all weaponry training. Hanbo (short staff) teaches the use of *STICK* based weapons, defined as being anything of a solid nature that emphasize thrusting and striking as well as methods of locking the joints during grappling. Tanto (dagger) teaches the use of *BLADE* based weapons, defined as anything with a cutting edge or sharp point that emphasize stabbing and slashing as well as methods of using the pommel. Kusari Fundo (short chain) teaches the use of *FLEXIBLE* based weapons, defined as being anything of a pliable nature that emphasize flailing as well as various methods of entangling. The Kugi (spikes) teaches the use of *PROJECTILE* based weapons, defined as anything that can be thrown or shot that emphasize striking or stabbing as well as methods of pressure point attack during grappling.

SHURIKENJUTSU - THROWING BLADES

The art of throwing blades dates far back into Japan's history when a princely warrior initiated an attack by hurling his *Hashi* (chopsticks) at his enemy. The attack proved to be very effective and has since become known as "Shurikenjutsu," which translates as "The blade behind the hand," implying that a throwing weapon is best used as a tool of surprise to either gain initiative or ensure escape. Rarely has a shuriken been accredited with actually killing an adversary, and in the situations in which death did occur, it was most likely due to a lethal coating of poison rather than the blade itself. The Kurai Kotori Ninja uses various throwing blade designs, but the cross (juji) half moon (hangetsu), spike (kugi), and four pointed (shippo) are preferred. However, beyond weapons specifically designed the be thrown, the Ninja can turn almost anything into a deadly projectile.

STAVES AND CLUBS

Bojutsu (staff combat) is based around fighting with poles made of wood, bamboo, or rattan of varying lengths. But the Bojutsu art contains a wide variety of powerful bludgeoning weapons. Large weapons such as a hammer (kanazuchi), studded staff (konsaibo), iron staff (tetsubo), oar (kai), and mace (tsuchiboko) are very effective in battle-field scenarios. In closer range situations, weapons like the iron fan (tesson), iron truncheon (jutte), spinning rods (shobo), small stick (hananegi), palm stick (kobo), iron fist (tekkon), fighting ring (bankokuchoki), forearm and shin guards (kote and sune) and shield (kame) are more effective. These and many other striking weapons provide the Ninja with the ability to inflict blunt trauma impacts that can shatter bones and inflict concussive damage on opponents.

HALBERDS

Even though the sword is a formidable weapon, the halberd proved to be its better during battlefield campaigns. The Kurai Kotori Ninja utilizes three primary designs. The straight bladed halberd (nagimaki), the curve bladed halberd (naginata), and the heavy bladed halberd (bisento). These weapons were designed in such a way that the Ninja could still employ fluid sword-like techniques while remaining at a safer distance, which is the true value of any polearm, whether halberd, staff or spear. If properly employed, these weapons could dominate a conflict, allowing the wielder to focus more on offensive maneuvers with less need for defensive techniques. One mighty slash could effectively sever limbs or destroy armor.

CHAINS AND FLAILS

Chains and flails are extremely valuable because of their concealability combined with their effectiveness when used to flail, strike and/or entangle. When flailed properly, a weighted end gains vast momentum that generates immense power that can shatter bones. The primary weapon of the system is a 6' to 9' weighted chain (o-kusari). This weapon is very effective against swordsmen because the chain's length allows the wielder to stay beyond the reach of the blade while its weighted end is brought down against the swordsmen's wrists. The O-kusari is usually flailed in an effort to keep the enemy at bay, then when an opening becomes available, the chain is whipped out into its attack. Secondary weapons include the ball and chain (gekigan), chain whip (muchi kusari), chain bola (san kusari), sickle chain (nagegama), two sectional flail (ni setsu kon), and the three sectional flail (san setsu kon).

SICKLES AND AXES

Twin sickles (nichogama) are devastating tools. Their effectiveness lies in their ability to confuse the enemy with an endless array of hypnotic maneuvers coupled with the fact that they are used in pairs, allowing one to parry as the other attacks, which gives the Ninja the ability to use defensive and offensive fighting techniques simultaneously. Because of the way the blades are attached to the shafts of these weapons, they are also capable of complex trapping and manipulating techniques.   Other mid-range weapons taught within the system include deeply curved sickles (natagama), small sickles (kogama), twin axe (masakari), and hatchet (te ono).   There are also two larger weapons taught in the kamajutsu system.   The great sickle (ogama), and great axe (o-no), both of which are too heavy and bulky to be wielded in pairs.

SPEAR

Being on the receiving end of a well aimed spear thrust is like being the recipient of a deadly poison.   This is because the three sided spear (sankakuyari) has a uniquely designed triangular blade that delivers wounds that do not close, making even the most minor injuries result in a slow painful death due to constant blood loss. Aside from the triangular bladed design, there are numerous other spear designs used by the Ninja.   The hook bladed spear (kamayari) was designed to trap and control the enemy's weapon and limbs.   The open bladed spear (hokoyari) resembles the inside curve of a crescent moon. The pendulum spear (furikoyari) has a circular blade that is capable of delivering potent sweeping attacks.   The short bladed spear (shakujoyari) has a shaft that is heavily fortified like a staff and small double edged blade that is used for quick thrusts and slashes.

CORDS AND NETS

The little known art of using cords and nets is invaluable to the Ninja operative. The main reason these weapons are so effective lies in their concealability. Even though they appear to be less ferocious than other weapons, this only serves to make their amazing trapping and whipping techniques more surprising. These weapons are endowed with the ability to entangle limbs, disarm weapons and constrict breath. They are the ultimate tools of silent elimination. The primary weapon in the system is the silken cord (torinawa) which is used to entangle and restrain an opponent. Other weapons include the large net (o-toami) wielded by two or more Ninja, the mid-sized net (chu-toami), used by a single Ninja, the net whip (muchi-toami), used as a companion weapon to a sword or short spear, and the rope and hook (kaginawa) used in both combat and as a climbing tool.

BOW AND CROSSBOW

The bow and arrow are among the first weapons employed by the military caste in Japan. Kyubajutsu (the way of the bow and the horse) is recorded in some of Japan's earliest historical texts. During its early applications, the bow and arrow were used primarily as an aggressive weapon employed by Kyubasen (mounted archers) and Tohosen (foot archers) by firing at opponents at close range. However, in later years the archers took a more defensive position, firing their arrows in a volley type fashion, creating a rain of razor tipped shafts. One main aspect that has always remained the same in the art of the Hankyu (short bow) is that of discipline. Only those with a calm and resolute spirit are said to possess the ability to launch an arrow with spiritual guidance. The other weapon in the system is the crossbow (jujikakyu).

BLOWGUNS AND DARTS

Blowguns (fukidake) and darts (fukiya) are one of the Ninja's favorite methods of attacking an enemy. A well placed shot could inject lethal doses of poison into the bloodstream of an unwary victim, hinder a pursuer, or cause an enemy's horse to rear up when hit by the invisible projectile. The reason this is a preferred weapon is due to the fact that the Ninja does not have to face a skilled opponent directly. Why chance a defeat at the hands of a superior armed and armored foe when a small air-guided missile could be accurately shot from a distance. This art is often combined with learning to make plant, animal, and synthetic poisons (dokujutsu).

COMBINATION WEAPONS

In Ninjutsu there are various tools that involve two or more weapon skills. The Kyoketsushayoge (rope knife) is a tool that encompasses a knife (tanto), a hooked blade (kama), a rope (torinawa) and a heavy metal ring (bankokuchoki). The Kusarigama (sickle and chain) is a tool that combines the lethal close range sickle (kama) with a long weighted chain (kusari) to create a multi-range weapon. Other combination weapons include, short staff and chain (chigiriki), staff and flail (bo karazao), staff with concealed chain (feruzue) and staff with concealed blade (shikomizue). Each aspect of these weapons must be studied individually before the they can effectively be used. In this manner the warrior learns about each weapons strengths and weaknesses, which in turn enables them to use each piece to its full potential when they are combined.

SWORD RESTRAINMENT WEAPONS

The sword, being the main weapon of the Japanese warrior-caste, provided the Ninja with an interesting challenge. That challenge was to come up with weapons that could hinder or restrain a swordsmans ability to fight.   Even though any of the Ninja's primary weapons could provide them with reliable self-protection, it was the development of sword restrainment tools that greatly increased the their ability to ward off the lightning fast blade of the Samurai. Among these specialized weapons were the iron truncheon (jutte), man-catcher (sasumata), t-staff (tsukabo), sleeve entangler (sodegarami), and tiger claws (torashuko), however, there are many more unique tools that made it possible to exploit weaknesses in the Samurai's deadly weapon and protective vestments.

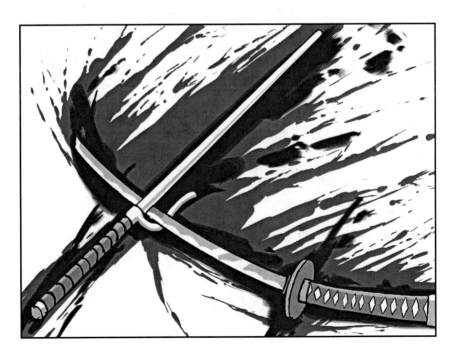

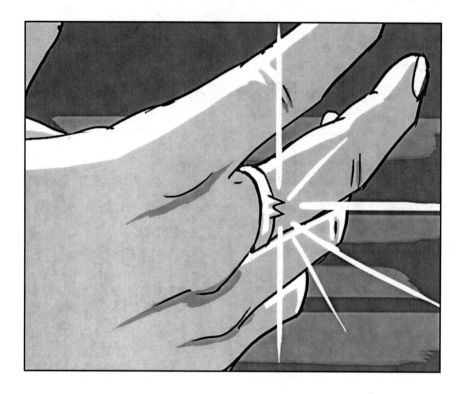

HIDDEN WEAPONS

Hidden weapons are a Ninja specialty. Using common objects as weapons and concealing secret devices that can later be employed against the enemy requires a strong sense of insight and planning. A good hidden weapon is one that can be in plain sight yet offers no noticeable threat to those who perceive it. With this in mind, the Kurai Kotori Ninja begin their quest to devise weapons that are virtually undetectable, such as the spiked ring (kakute), poison needle (dokubari), garrote (nawa fundo), wooden comb (kushi), folding fan (senssu), blinding powder (metsubishi), umbrella (kasa), cat claws (nekote), wooden clogs (geta), chopsticks (hashi), prayer beads (juzu), sash, (obi), and many more improvised tools.

FIREARMS AND CANNONS

The Ninja's use of fire and explosives is legendary. Disappearing in a cloud of smoke or igniting explosive devices to cause destruction are among the Ninja's greatest tactics. Ninja utilized these skills from the moment they acquired the appropriate chemicals from the Mongols in the late 1200's, so it should be no surprise that a Ninja would embrace the use of firearms and cannons when they became available in the mid 1500's. The length of the barrel determined the accuracy of the weapon. Although a long musket (jozutsu) would be superior as a sniping weapon from long distances, the Ninja often preferred shorter muskets (chuzutsu) or small handguns (tanzutsu) for more intimate encounters. Beyond these firearms, the Ninja also made hand cannons (sodezutsu) that were not very accurate, but their blast radius was wide, making them effective against more than one enemy at a time.

STEALTH

It is often said that the Ninja is a supreme master of stealth, able to vanish at will or change into a wild animal form in order to disappear. In actuality it is the Ninja's understanding of invisibility that gives them the advantage. Invisibility in reality is simply knowing how to fool the enemies senses in order to remain undetected, much like a magician misdirects in order to mystify and confuse. To accomplish these feats, the Ninja must learn specialized techniques of moving quietly (kage-aruki), running skills (hayagakejutsu), crawling (hofukujutsu), create false sounds (gionjutsu), and using trained animals (dobutsujutsu), combined with a strong understanding of human scope of vision. Beyond these skills, a Ninja must also be mentally prepared to have a quiet, undetectable mind (kage-shin) to mask their intentions.

CONCEALMENT

Although all Ninja are taught to be stealthy and well versed in invisibility tactics, there is always the possibility that they will be detected. In this situation the Ninja must be able to effectively hide. These methods of disappearance are based on earth (chigakure), making use of rocks, dirt and man-made structures. Water (suigakure), making use of streams, ponds or lakes. Fire (kagakure), making use of light, flame, smoke and explosives. Wind (kazegakure), making use of wind, snow, fog, and rain. Lastly and perhaps the most effective, Celestial (hensogakure), making use of anything that can alter the physical appearance of the Ninja so they can disappear in plain sight by assuming the identity and attributes of person that is less likely to be noticed.

ESCAPE

The Ninja must study their enemy's leaders and strategists in an attempt to determine what type battlefield tactics they are most likely to encounter on their mission. By thinking in this fashion, the Ninja can devise a variety of escape plans that actually work against the tactics used by the enemy's troops. This provides the Ninja with the ability to stay one step ahead of their pursuers. Avoiding terrain that leaves tracks, setting traps, hiding weapon and supply caches, and leading the enemy into pre-planned ambushes are all valid tactics. It may take many months of studying the activities of the enemy before the Ninja begins seeing patterns to their actions, but the amount of time is irrelevant. In the end, the Ninja will know more about the enemy than the enemy knows about themselves.

RECONNAISSANCE AND INFILTRATION

In the complex arts of reconnaissance (teisatsujutsu) and infiltration (sennyujutsu) a Ninja is taught to scout out the enemies fortifications, memorize the strengths and weaknesses of its layout, gain information from locals and relay that and any other pertinent information back to the clan. Ninja reconnaissance teams are also used to scout out potential battlefields long before a battle was to occur. They would then deliver a detailed map showing all of the predominant land contours that would shed light on how troops could best be deployed. When infiltrating an area or structure, the Ninja must know the schedule of everyone who operates within the target zone, the areas with the least traffic, and physical obstacles that bar their path, and if there are any potential allies that could be enlisted to assist.

SURVIVAL SKILLS

Seizonjutsu, the art of survival, is of the utmost importance to a Ninja. The ability to survive in the wilderness was not a luxury, it was a necessity. Most Ninja conducted their activities from remote mountain and forest regions in an effort to remain undetected by those who would oppose them. Living in this environment made Ninja extremely rugged and resourceful. Important factors include having proper clothing, a water source, fire building capability, an understanding of makeshift shelters, cutting tools, light source, non-perishable food creation, knowledge of plant and animal resources and creating a base camp in a defensible area with viable escape routes.

GROUP TACTICS

The art of group tactics (senjojutsu) is a large part of combative operations. This training enhances a Ninja on many levels, especially those pertaining to teamwork. Senjojutsu tactics are usually employed by a strike force of five to seven Ninja. Although small by battlefield standards, these elite teams are highly efficient at carrying out a variety of objectives without being detected. Thus emphasizing that stealth is preferable to direct engagement with the enemy. The variables that a team can face in the field are countless, so the team must be tested with constant mission simulations in order to hone their reflexes to perfection. Each one of the Ninja on these teams possess specialized skills, tools and weapons that makes them more effective as a group.

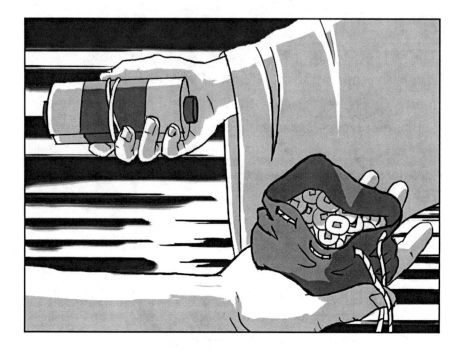

ESPIONAGE TACTICS

Learning to manipulate the world around them is the key to being an effective agent. A Ninja must be able to analyze their enemy's character at a moments notice to discover any weaknesses that can be exploited. This same analytical process to the environment in which the enemy is operating is valid. Once the Ninja understands their enemy and their resources they can begin creating events that cause the enemy to do what the Ninja wants without ever realizing it, and even if they find out, it will likely be too late to make any difference. Building false friendships, recruiting pawns, inciting betrayal among allies, releasing false information, or any other such action that causes the enemy to fall into the Ninja's web of illusion.

PSYCHOLOGICAL WARFARE

The Ninja is as much a psychological warrior as they are a physical warrior. The Ninja must become like a spectre in the enemies mind. Ultimately, the Ninja seeks out any mental weaknesses in their enemy that can be exploited. If no weaknesses are evident, the Ninja must create one for them through the use of special methods of mental manipulation known as Saiminjutsu, or The way of hypnosis. A Ninja must learn to apply the spectre in the mind tactic without exposing their intentions. The enemy should be totally unaware of any manipulation until it's too late. In ancient times, Ninja were often depicted as being in league with demonic forces, which caused their enemies to view them as supernatural entities.

MYSTICISM

Gorin Kuji Myo Himitsu Shaku, or the *Secret Knowledge of Inner Strength*, makes use of indepth medative techniques that are focused on unleashing the dormant spiritual powers that dwell deep within every Ninja.   If the Ninja can successfully tap into their inner power, they can accomplish superhuman feats.   Feats such as heightening mental and physical strength, healing abilities, directing spiritual energy, projecting thoughts and emotions and tapping into the realm of the shadow.   As mysterious as this sounds, these powers exist within every human being.   They are not magical energies as much as they are personal, spiritual energies that, if focused, can bring about the creation of powerful skills that breach the realm of normal human abilities.

THEATRICAL COMBAT

Chambara is the Japanese term for a unique genre of action film that glorified Japan's Feudal era. What made these films so unique is that they not only told entertaining stories, they also maintained realistic combat. These performed fighting skills were not faked by clever camera techniques because the actors were actually talented practitioners of swordsmanship. The arts depicted on screen had no ties to the competitive styles studied today, but were based on highly effective combative arts thats sole purpose was the efficient elimination of one's opponent. These films were the perfect medium to tell tales inspired by the heroic exploits of majestic *Samurai*, the lonely and tragic paths of the masterless *Ronin* and the deceptive and mysterious deeds of the ghost-like *Ninja*. Many Kurai Kotori Ninjutsu practitioners are also Chambara artists.

MODERN TECHNOLOGY

Mirai Shinobi, or *Future Ninja,* is a term that refers to a Ninja who is also skilled with modern weapons and tactics. Handguns, rifles, smoke grenades, tasers, liquid eye irritants, restrainment devices, body armor, survival implements, surveillance equipment, lock picking tools, and anything else available in the modern world that are adapted seamlessly into the Ninja's core art.

CHAPTER THREE

ETIQUETTE

CHAPTER THREE
ETIQUETTE

Reishiki, or "Etiquette," is a valuable aspect of martial training. To the uninitiated observer, Reishiki appears to be a method of making students subservient to instructors. However, the use of etiquette in the Dojo has nothing to do with such things. Reishiki is used to organize the dojo into a functional society, demonstrating discipline, dedication, development, common sense, and most of all manners.

TRANSLATION

Reishiki comes from two Japanese words. The first is "Rei" which is defined as: bow, salutation, salute, courtesy, propriety, ceremony, thanks and appreciation. The second part of the term is "Shiki" which is defined as: ceremony, rite or function. Combined, the term "Reishiki" translates as: Ceremonial manners.

EASTERN THOUGHT / WESTERN EYES

In the eyes of a Westerner, Reishiki must seem to be a curious phenomenon, but deeper inspection is needed to fully grasp its significance. Some people ask "What has all this ritual to do with learning to fight?" My answer is....everything. The first purpose of Reishiki is to place the mind in a proper state so it can be more efficiently taught *how* to learn.

THE ESSENCE OF REISHIKI

During a student's training, Reishiki takes on important and progressively deeper purposes. It is an inseparable part of Shugyo (warrior cultivation). It is used to test a student's willingness to submit their ego to destruction. As such, it becomes the foundation on which one tempers the soul of the warrior. But of course we don't actually destroy a student's ego. We instead aim to polish and mold the student's ego through hardship, challenge and reflection.

SELF-SACRIFICE

Acceptance or rejection of proper Reishiki can be utilized to expose a student's dedication or shortcomings to a Sensei (teacher). The student who constantly questions or refuses to embrace Reishiki is not suitable for continued training because they ultimately view their own opinions and desires as superior to the aims of the Ryu. Blinded by their own self-absorption, a student disrespectful of Reishiki is incapable of accepting the fact that their responsibility as a student is foremost to the Ryu (clan) and the benefit of others before themselves.

ETIQUETTE BREEDS SUCCESS

The experiences gained through Reishiki along with the technical execution of the skills of the Ryu merge into one singular expression. This combination of mental and physical experiences ultimately transform the soul. The increased sensitivity resulting from continued warrior cultivation allows the student to peer into their own heart in a way never before experienced. It is an epiphany of sorts for many. Responsibility to the Ryu, to their seniors, and to humanity at large become more important than fulfilling their own selfish desires. In this way a benevolent spirit is forged and wisdom is free to flourish. Abstract concepts of life and death place the student's existence in the proper natural context. The transcendence of the spirit world often presents itself for the first time. Over the many years of forging the student becomes one with the world as well as to the place where the spirits of our ancestors reside. Without this sensitivity and the increased awareness of their proper place in the world, a martial artist can lose their way and develop a distorted moral code, a code that justifies ego driven self-gratification and rationalized violence. The wisdom gained through proper Reishiki is protection from the *Kami* or "deities" against the evil that humanity has wrestled with for generations. That evil is malevolent violence, a curse that is the bane of human existence.

ETIQUETTE GUIDELINES
Students should take care to study the following etiquette guidelines. These rules serve as the foundation for how the Kurai Kotori clan operates in a training environment and students should maintain them with vigilance.

<u>ENTERING THE DOJO</u>

1. Arrive on time for training. If you are consistently late without reason it is unacceptable.

2. Upon entering the Dojo, the student should remove their shoes before proceeding into the training area.

Outdoor shoes are not allowed on the training floor

3. When entering or exiting the Dojo, the student should always bow towards the Kamiza (dojo shrine) side of the Dojo. If there is no shrine, simply bow when entering and exiting the entrance.

4. Always greet your instructor when you first show up for training to let them know you have arrived and are eager for instruction.

5. A common term upon meeting your instructor is "Osu!" In Japanese the word is comprised of two characters. The first character is defined as "Push." The second character is defined as "Endure." It is used as a greeting of great respect and can also be used to replace words and phrases such as "yes," "all right," "good," "I will do it," "I will try hard," and "excuse me." In fact a student is expected to never say "Hello" to his seniors but say "OSU" instead. At its most profound it's a plea deep inside a person

to overcome the frailties of the human condition. The single word expresses the philosophy of Ninjutsu. A good student is expected to have the "Spirit of Osu." This is the underlying force of tradition which affects the Ninja practitioner's execution of duties, physical training and human interaction.

UNIFORM AND EQUIPMENT

1. All uniforms are to be properly tailored. Sleeves will be cut to just below the elbow and pants will be securely fastened at the calf with leg ties. The family crest (patch) will be sewn on the uniform on the left chest over the heart. Uniforms must be kept clean and free of wrinkles.

2. Dressing room etiquette - Black belts and upper ranks should be allowed to change first at the end of class. Lower ranking students should wait quietly outside the respective dressing rooms for their turn. Never leave anything in the dressing room. Students should bring their gear to the Dojo and take their gear home with them on a per class basis.

3. Students will not put on their leg ties or tie belts in the Dojo. These items should be on prior to exiting the dressing room.

4. All equipment, including practice weapons, safety gear, armor or any other such gear used in training are to be obtained from Dojo sources.

5. The student is responsible for having all weapons and equipment required by their rank. The Dojo is not responsible for providing these materials for student use. If the student continually shows up without the necessary gear, they will not be allowed to participate.

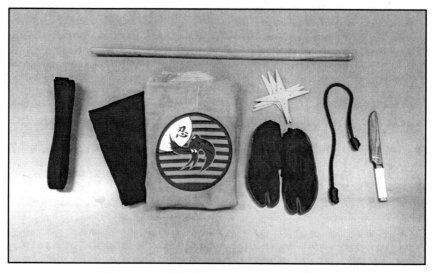

Always have basic weapons and equipment

PREPARATION FOR TRAINING

1. <u>There should be no unsupervised practicing before class so that others do not have to dodge anything while making their way to and from the changing rooms</u>. To practice, especially with weaponry, without being instructed to do so is very disrespectful.

2. Once changed, the student should take a seat to the side with the appropriate training equipment and await the start of class or begin light stretching to prepare the body for training.

3. When in the Dojo, the student should never lean on their weapons or against the wall. This is an outward show of laziness. Stand tall and be attentive of the information that is being presented.

4. There are two ways to sit in the Dojo. One is to sit in "Seiza," or "Kneeling" Posture. The second is to sit in "Fudoza," or "Cross-legged" posture. Never lie down on the floor unless you are injured.

5. When the command "Seiretsu" is given, all students should line up facing the Kamiza according to rank. (If a sword is being used, it will be held by the scabbard in the right hand just below the guard. The pommel will point to the rear with the blade tip forward, cutting edge down).

6. When the command "Sabate" is given, all students will kneel down into Seiza position. (If a sword is being used, it is placed on the student's right side, pommel forward, cutting edge outward).

7. When the command "Sensei ni rei" is given, all students will place their right hand to the ground in front of them followed by their left hand. The pointer fingers of each hand should be touching with the thumbs overlapping to create a triangle opening between the hands. The student then bows forward. The teacher will return the bow. Students will not rise until the teacher has risen from their bow. As the student rises, their left hand is drawn into their lap followed by their right.

8. The teacher will turn to face the Kamiza. When the command "Zarei" is given, both teacher and students will bow toward the Kamiza. The students will not rise from their bow until the teacher rises. (If a sword is being used, it will be placed in front of the student prior to bowing, pommel to the right, cutting edge forward).

9. When the command "Mokuso" is given, the students will place the back of their left hand into the palm of their right hand and lower their gaze to sit in quiet meditation.

Quiet thought

10. After a moment of silence, the teacher will rise to a standing position and turn to face the students.

11. When the command "Sodachi" is given, students will rise to a standing position. To stand properly, the student will first retract their feet so their toes are pressing the ground beneath their hips. The student will then raise their right leg up to their right side and use it to push their body up into a standing position. (If a sword is being used,

the student will grasp it with their right hand beneath the guard and lift the sword to a vertical position to their side as they rise. Once standing, the sword is transferred to the left hand and held horizontally at waist level or placed in the belt).

12. When the command "Gasso" is given, both teacher and students will place their hands palms together in front of their chest and bow forward at the waist. (If a sword is being used, the student will maintain its position in their left hand and lift the right hand to perform the salute).

DURING TRAINING

1. It is imperative that you inform the instructor of any physical ailment you might have prior to training. If an injury is significant, it is suggested that a strip of red cloth be tied on the injured limb so other students and instructors are reminded to avoid the area. If the injury is on the torso, the strip of cloth can be tied to the belt.

2. <u>If a class is already in progress, kneel off to the side and wait to be called in to join.</u> If you must leave before class is over make sure you let the instructor know before hand that you need to leave early. Bow to your partner, then bow out and leave the training area. Get dressed and leave quietly, making sure not to disturb any other classmates. It is never okay to continually arrive late or leave classes before they are officially dismissed.

3. When training alone (tandoku renshu) or when all students are lined up to perform acrobatic drills, striking drills, footwork exercises, or any other type of solitary action, the instructor will begin with the command "Yoi!" or "Ready!" Students will respond with the phrase "Yosh!" in a very strong, focused tone. In most cases these exercises will be done in sets of ten. On the tenth maneuver, the student should execute a strong "Kiai!".

4. When an instructor demonstrates a technique, or shows an additive or variable, the student should watch and listen closely. When asked to perform the lesson, the students should respond in unison with "Hai!" or "Yes!" Another acceptable response is "Osu!"

5. When two students work together (sotai renshu) there will always be a defender (Tori) and an attacker (Uke). The Uke will apply an aggressive action and the Tori will respond with prearranged maneuvers designed to counter the attack. The relationship between these students is one of collaboration, not opposition. Uke is not trying to truly hurt Tori, they are trying to help Tori learn through the repetition of technique. This partnership is one of mutual respect. When working in a group, the highest ranking student will be Tori (defender) with next highest rank assuming the role of Uke (attacker).

6. When joint locks, throws, or other such immobilizing techniques are applied, the likelihood of physical pain should be expected. The proper response is for Uke to tap

the ground with their hand in a fashion that demonstrates the technique is working. If the hands are not free to tap, the verbal phrase "Itai!" or "It hurts!" is an appropriate response. Should you become injured, let the instructor know immediately and they will handle the situation. Other students should continue training unless they are asked to assist the injured party.

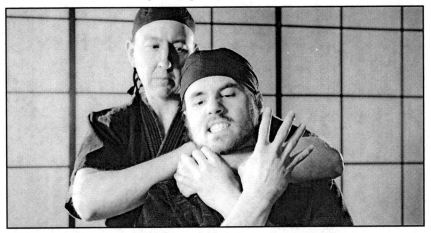

Tori (defender) ceases a technique when Uke (attacker) taps

7. Uke should never counter or disrupt Tori's technique unless instructed to do so. A teacher may ask Uke to offer differing levels of resistance to Tori as a means of testing Tori's ability to apply the technique.

8. At times students will be allowed to fight freely (jiyu renshu) in supervised striking and/or grappling contests. These may pit one student versus another, one student versus multiple opponents, or two or more allied students against multiple opponents. These matches are used to demonstrate the fact that things can change at a moments notice and how the student can adapt will determine their

effectiveness in a physical conflict. There is to be no sparring or other such partner training unless there is a supervising instructor.

9. <u>Never instruct another student while in the Dojo or outside the Dojo, unless specifically asked to do so</u>. The Dojo Headmaster (Jonin) is there for a reason, to instruct. It is the responsibility of the student to kneel down and wait for the Jonin to attend to their questions. This way there is no conflict of instruction. Just because a student has a black belt does not make them a resource for lower ranking students. Jonin will decide if any other black belt should assist in in a students instruction process.

AFTER TRAINING

1. When class is over...it's over. Students should refrain from unsupervised practice after class. If you are endowed with excess energy, you should clean the Dojo so it's prepared for the next days training.

2. It is the student's responsibility to keep the Dojo clean and neat. If a trash can is full, empty it. If the mats need cleaned, clean them, if the floor is dirty sweep it. The dojo is a reflection of you, and a disheveled Dojo means its members are lazy and uncaring. It is not a duty but a privilege to have a place to train in the ways of the warrior, so please maintain it with compassion and caring.

Cleaning the Dojo

AT SOCIAL EVENTS

1. Etiquette is not limited to dojo training.   Your teacher is your teacher, regardless of location.

GUEST INSTRUCTORS

1. Regardless of style or affiliation, any instructor who is brought in to teach students should be given the highest respect.   They may have chosen a different path, but their hard work and dedication should be admired.

LEADERSHIP / TEACHING CREDENTIALS

1. Teaching credentials are given to those who have diligently studied the theory and application of the skills and techniques maintained by the Kurai Kotori Clan and have achieved Black Belt III (Renshi).   Those who have attained such certification are required to maintain an open line of communication with the Hombu Dojo in a sincere

effort to stay up to date with any changes or additives to the training structure. Failure to do so nullifies the instructor's authority to officially represent the art.

2. Certified instructors should maintain their own training by visiting the Hombu Dojo or having the Jonin visit their respective school/location at least once a year. Although not mandatory, these visits are invaluable to continued growth.

3. Training sessions will contain comprehensive focus on Unarmed Combat, Acrobatics, Basic Weaponry and Swordsmanship. These four skills are considered the foundation of the Kurai Kotori system.

4. Specialized skills involving Advanced Weapons, Stealth, Invisibility, Mysticism, etc... will be taught in specialized training modules with specific time sensitive goals in which to accomplish the process.

5. No instructor, regardless of rank, should take it upon themselves to alter any training content, in written or verbal form, without written consent. Any changes within the overall clan structure will be initiated by the Hombu dojo and it falls upon the instructor to maintain them.

6. Any certified instructor can teach a student, but all rank advancements will be issued by the *Kurai Kotori Martial Arts Federation* under the authorization of the Jonin.

7. All instructors will provide their students with patches bearing the clan kamon that will be firmly sewn onto the left chest of their uniform. No other logo or image will take precedence over this family symbol.

8. No training materials will be created or distributed without the written consent of the Hombu Dojo. All relevant materials will be provided by the Hombu Dojo. All training materials will be assigned a version number and date so updates can be easily tracked.

TERMINOLOGY

Learning terminology is imperative in learning the art. Many Japanese letters sound the same as they do in English, but some letters are pronounced and written differently.

Japanese Sound	English Sound	Example
a	ah *(as in father)*	Aka *(ah-ka)*
ai	i *(as in eye)*	Kurai *(Koo-rai)*
e	ei *(as in ray)*	Yame *(yah-may)*
ei	ay *(as in day)*	Sensei *(sehn-say)*
i	ee *(as in key)*	Jonin *(joh-neen)*
o	oh *(as in go)*	Dojo *(doh-joh)*
oi	oy *(as in toy)*	Yoi *(yoy)*
u	oo *(as in boot)*	Ninjutsu *(nin-joot-soo)*
tsu	soo *(as in soon)*	Tsuki *(soo-key)*

THE CLAN / ARTS

1. Kurai Kotori Ryu - Clan of the Dark Lone Bird
2. Ninjutsu - Art of the Ninja
3. Kenjutsu - Art of the Sword
4. Chambara - Art of Theatrical Combat

TITLES / POSITIONS

1. Jonin - Leader / Headmaster
2. Jiki Deshi - Direct Apprentice
3. Kenshi - Sword master
4. Sensei - Teacher
5. Taisho - General / Leader of their own Dojo
6. Chunin - Sub-commander / Organizer
7. Genin - Field Agent / Student

UNIFORM / GARB

1. Mon - Family crest
2. Hakama - Pleated divided skirt / pants
3. Keikogi - Training jacket
4. Shinobi Shozuku - Classical Ninja uniform
5. Zukin - Shroud / Hood
6. Tekoh - Forearm sleeves
7. Kyahan - Leg wraps
8. Tabi - Split toe shoes
9. Obi - Belt / Sash
10. Kimo - Cord / Leg Ties
11. Gaito - Cloak

WEAPONS / EQUIPMENT

1. Katana - Long sword
2. Shinobigatana - Straight sword
3. Bokuto - Wooden sword
4. Chikuto - Bamboo sword
5. Hanbo - Three foot staff
6. Tanto - Knife
7. Kusari Fundo - Weighted chain
8. Shaken - Bladed wheel
9. Kugi - Throwing spikes

TRAINING

1. Seiretsu - Line up
2. Sabate - Sit
3. Sensei ni rei - Bow to the teacher
4. Zarei - Spiritual bow
5. Mokuso - Quiet thought
6. Sodachi - Stand up
7. Tori - Defender
8. Uke - Attacker
9. Yoi - Ready!
10. Kata - Prearranged form
11. Waza - Prearranged technique
12. Ie - No
13. Hai - Yes
14. Itai! - It hurts!
15. Yame - Stop

COUNTING

1. Ichi - One
2. Ni - Two
3. San - Three
4. Shi - Four
5. Go - Five
6. Roku - Six
7. Shichi - Seven
8. Hachi - Eight
9. Ku - Nine
10. Ju - Ten
11. Ju ichi - Eleven
12. Ju ni - Twelve
13. Ju san - Thirteen
14. Ju shi - Fourteen
15. Ju go - Fifteen
16. Ju roku - Sixteen
17. Ju shichi - Seventeen
18. Ju hachi - Eighteen
19. Ju ku - Nineteen
20. Ni ju - twenty
21. Ni ju ichi
22. Ni ju ni
23. Ni ju san
24. Ni ju shi
25. Ni ju go
26. Ni ju roku
27. Ni ju shichi
28. Ni ju hachi
29. Ni ju ku
30. San ju

DIRECTIONAL

1. Migi - Right
2. Hiadari - Left
3. Zenpo / Mae - Forward / Front
4. Koho / Ushiro - Back / Rear
5. Yoko - Side
6. Naname - Angular
7. Mawate - Turn
8. Omote - Outside
9. Ura - Inside

<u>CONVERSATIONAL</u>

1. Domo Arigato Gozaimas - Thank you very much
2. Do Itashimashita - You're welcome
3. Ohayo - Good morning
4. Konnichiwa - Good afternoon
5. Konbanwa - Good evening
6. Oyasuminasai - Good night
7. Sayonara - Goodbye

CHAPTER FOUR

VIRTUES, LAWS,
AND DOCTRINES

CHAPTER FOUR
VIRTUES, LAWS, AND DOCTRINES

The Kurai Kotori Ninja adhere to a specific set of virtues, laws, and doctrines that provide insight into how they should deal with the things they encounter in life. First are the *Virtues of the Ninja*. These virtues serve as the guidelines that dictate how the Ninja deals with their daily existence. Next there are the *Laws of the Ninja*. The laws serve the Ninja in times of conflict, setting the standard for how they deal with enemies. Finally, there are the *Doctrines of the Ninja*. The doctrines deal with the inner workings of the Ninja's existence and are used to stimulate deeper vision into the powers that shape one's destiny.

VIRTUES OF THE NINJA

There are six specific *virtues* that the Ninja adheres to. These virtues teach the Ninja how to deal with *clan*, *family* and *personal* situations.

GIRI - DUTY
Giri is best described as the Ninja's "Obligation" to the clan. There are no limits to the Ninja's service. Although extreme by American standards, Giri is maintained to ensure prosperity. If Giri is present in the clan, the clan will prosper. This is because the clan's objective is the individual Ninja's objective as well. With such unity, nothing is impossible.

SHIKI - RESOLUTE

Shiki dictates that the Ninja be firm in reaching their objectives, willing to suffer any hardship or indignity to succeed. When a Ninja sets out on a mission, they must not fail.

FUDO - STRENGTH

The concept of Fudo means that the Ninja must maintain a strong body and mind. This is of extreme importance, for any weakness, physical or mental, can be exploited by an enemy.

DORYO - MAGNANIMITY

Anyone who wields great power must use it wisely. It is at this point that the Ninja must remember that having the ability to kill does not necessarily justify using it. To remain a true warrior, one must understand the importance of mercy.

ONSHA - GENEROSITY

To prosper on the path, one must come to understand the importance of giving. Using one's skills to aid others is truly honorable. To be unselfish in word and deed not only brings honor to the Ninja, but also the clan they serve.

NINYO - CHIVALROUS

Ninyo dictates that when a conflict arises, the Ninja should not hesitate to act. It is at this point that the Ninja must decide what warrants the use of their skills when interfering in the affairs of others.

LAWS OF THE NINJA

There are four *laws* that the Ninja uses when preparing for battle. These laws allow the Ninja the freedom to do whatever is necessary to defeat their opponent.

ANONYMITY

The Ninja must always keep his true thoughts and actions unknown to his enemies. Such secrecy is important in the Ninja's planning stages. Even those close to the Ninja are not privileged to information concerning a mission. The fewer who know anything the better.

EXPLOITATION

The Ninja must take advantage of anything and everything to defeat his enemy. To accomplish this, the Ninja studies every aspect of his enemies existence. The purpose of this information gathering is to find and exploit every possible avenue.

TRICKERY

The Ninja must always keep his enemies confused to what is real and what is illusion. In doing this, the enemy never knows what to expect, and if they don't know what to expect, they can't prepare a defense.

STRATEGY

The Ninja never acts with random emotion. Strategy is the key to success. The Ninja must devise various plans of action, and each plan must have a contingency. Not only must the Ninja win, they must do it with style.

DOCTRINES OF THE NINJA

There are a myriad of *doctrines* maintained by the Kurai Kotori clan. These teachings have been passed down from family to family in many of Japan's Martial Traditions.

MICHI

Michi translates as the "Path." The path of the Ninja is to cultivate body, mind and spirit throughout their existence. This cultivation is often times referred to as "Musha Shugyo," or "Warrior Cultivation." Even though it sounds quite mystical, there is no room for failure in its attainment. In the past, Musha Shugyo was accomplished by traveling to different Bujutsu schools and challenging the top student to combat. Through this action the Ninja experienced combat in its rawest form, where they either won, or they died. Even though this type of action seems extreme, the

Shugyo

concept behind it is quite ingenious. By placing oneself in such an intense situation one would surely acquire a heightened awareness in combat. This acute sense that the Ninja developed through Musha Shugyo trained them to deal with the enemy as quickly as possible, never taking chances that would alter their ability to win.

In the Kurai Kotori Ryu the concept of Musha Shugyo still represents an important factor in the Ninja's training. It teaches the Ninja to take full advantage of all situations, never taking anything for granted. In every combat scenario the Ninja should have "Seishi o choetsu," or the "Transcending thoughts of life and death," knowing that they must savor all their moments in life so that upon dying they can leave the physical realm with the knowledge that they used all of their life's gifts to their full extent.

Life and Death

NAKA-IMA

To remain powerful, the Ninja must constantly expand their awareness. This is the only way to lead a plentiful life. New and old compliment one another, but each remain separate entities. The only way to integrate them as one is to envision all things as being part of the "Eternal now," or "Forever present" concept. This concept dictates that the warrior arts are mastered by giving regard to the exponents of past ages combined with the information available today. However, it should be known that if the art is to flourish, the new can never cover the old.

NIN

The concept of "Nin" is often referred to as both "Perseverance" and "Strength," but what it really comes down to is "Mental Attitude." This attitude is what separates the Ninja from the average Martial artist. The Ninja's mental state is reflected in the goals they set for

themselves. To become a master of unarmed combat is only one of their concerns, they must also attain mastery with all weapons, become proficient at making poisons, elixirs and explosives, able to pass unnoticed while in disguise, attain grace at climbing, stealth and acrobatics, and become accomplished in survival

Perseverance

skills, concealment and infiltration tactics. These are just a few of the Ninja's objectives among countless others. What it all comes down to is the growth. Anything that is going to offer the Ninja insight into themselves is part of the Kurai Kotori Tradition.

SHIBUMI

Once the Ninja becomes knowledgeable in many areas, they enter a state known as "Shibumi," which is better referred to as "Simplicity" of both body and mind. When Shibumi comes into effect, the Ninja moves with unmatched elegance, making even the most complex of things appear to be a simple feat requiring little thought.

KI

Ki is the "Energy" that exists in all living things. It cannot be seen or touched, it simply exists. Ki is evident when one's mind and body are working together in total harmony. Even though the development of Ki is not an easy task, it must be accomplished if one wishes to tap into his or her true power.

The first thing the Ninja should focus on is the proper execution of physical technique, for if the body becomes balanced and controlled the Ninja's Ki will begin to develop. Physical training must be completed before mental training can occur. Many Ninja are so engulfed with the thought of attaining a strong energy that they become obsessed with the idea. They want to fly past the physical training and learn the secret mystical chant that will give them access to supreme power. Such power is only available to those who cultivate their life energy patiently and diligently.

The same method of self-concentration used to train the Ninja physically can be used in the beginning stages of training the mind. Awareness is the main point of focus, learning to notice the smallest of details in all things. Throughout the Ninja's mental training he should learn to appreciate such art forms as calligraphy, painting, pottery, carpentry and theatre, because through these methods of artistic expression the Ninja acquires knowledge that requires self-concentration and commitment to the finest detail.

HARA

Ki is passed through the "Hara," or "Stomach region." This is the most powerful area in the Ninja's body, for it houses the center of Ki deep within. This inner area is known as the "Seika no itten," or "Vital point," and it is considered to be where the mind and body unite, creating the strongest emanation of balanced energy within the body. The Hara is utilized when the Ninja allows all their life force to sink to their vital point. When this is accomplished, the mind and body are as one, which enable the Ninja's energy to emerge focused and controlled.

KIAI

Kiai translates as "Intense energy," and it is often interpreted as a mere yell during the Ninja's attack. However, Kiai houses a much deeper meaning. Kiai can actually be described as being raw emotion, the Ninja's spirit unleashed upon the physical realm. Many arts stress Kiai because it forces one to breathe during the application of the techniques, but this is definitely not the full potential of Kiai.

There are specific sounds that are released, depending on what type of action is being taken by the Ninja. If the Ninja is attacking, their Kiai screams up from their Hara and creates a type of "Ei" sound. If the Ninja's attack is successful their Kiai will transform into "Ei-yah," which signifies "Zanshin," or "Remaining spirit" after a good technique. However, if the Ninja is struck or thrown, they should let out a receiving Kiai that makes the sound "Toh," which armors their body to absorb impact. Yet this is still not the full extent of Kiai. The Kurai Kotori clan also uses a Kiai that emits no audible noise. This is called a *concealed shout*, and it's used to focus one's energy silently. True Kiai can be felt by all when demonstrated by one who has practiced their craft for many years. It is the feeling they emit, a feeling that separates them from others. They are able to capture your attention with their every move.

AIKI

Aiki is "Internal energy," and it signifies harmony from within the Ninja. This energy emanates from the Ninja, projecting a calm and confident spirit that can penetrate the enemy's mind, destroying their will to fight.

The attainment of Aiki cannot be forced, it simply happens. In essence, Aiki is the method of dominating the enemy with the spirit alone, where a simple glance is all that is needed to utterly defeat anyone who stands in the path of the Ninja's objective.

IN AND YO

The concept of In and Yo (yin and yang) plays an important part in the Ninja's way of life. This is because from within its depths the Ninja gains the knowledge that there is a total balance between the positive and negative forces of the universe. In gaining this knowledge the Ninja can see things as a whole, realizing that both In and Yo have equal importance in the overall scheme.

Knowing that good and evil, right and wrong, and light and dark are simply two different views of the same thing is what gives the Ninja the upper hand. They understand that there is only balance and imbalance. The Ninja must work in accordance with In and Yo to adjust any imperfections within its structure. This is to say that if one becomes stronger than the other the Ninja should recognize the imbalance and attempt to correct it.

The balance can be seen in the internal workings of nature. The sun and the moon never cease their function of rising and setting and rising again, giving us both light and darkness without thought. However, if the sun were to become predominant over the moon, the planetary system would shift, and life as we know it would cease to exist. Even though this is a grand scale example of balance, it is the same in all things. No matter how simple it may seem... balance must be maintained.

In and Yo

When applying In and Yo to combat it should be known that the balance lies within the combatants involved. What determines the winner over the loser is not based on who is right or wrong, or good or bad, because these factors have little effect on the actual outcome of a conflict. Success in battle is solely based on skill and planning. Never confuse yourself to this reality.

CHAPTER FIVE

PHILISOPHICAL
FOUNDATIONS

CHAPTER FIVE
PHILOSOPHICAL FOUNDATIONS

To obtain the true spirit of the warrior, the members of the Kurai Kotori clan are taught to envision all of their training adventures as taking place in the vastness of a spiritual forest. To intensify this visualization, the members of the clan view themselves as being one of the many creatures that dwell within the confines of the forest. By maintaining this mind set, the Ninja can come to understand that they are a part of the natural balance, a single piece of a much larger puzzle. The significance of the forest mentality is evident when one looks to its inhabitants. There are a multitude of creatures who exist within the forests boundaries. Each animal is uniquely different. So too is

The Forest of Insight

every Ninja. *Individuality* is the secret of the forest. Without such diversity, there would be no conflict, and without conflict, one would have no need to become a warrior. Unfortunately, a world without conflict is unnatural. As long as man has existed there has been war, from large scale battles between countries to civil wars to arguments between individuals. The reasons behind this fighting are irrelevant. The lesson is not. One must simply remember: *In all things there is opposition.*

Such opposition exists in nature as well. However, the Ninja who resides in the spiritual forest attempts to accept the concept of opposition. Every creature in the forest has what are considered to be natural enemies. This is a simple truth. Even creatures that pose no visible threat to others are prime targets for opposition. Just because the creature is passive by nature does not mean those around him adhere to the same method of existence. For example, just because the wild deer lives in a manner that poses no threat to the other animals in the forest does not mean that the mountain lion that stalks him will reconsider making a meal of him. It's all a matter of instinct. The hunter and the hunted. Each of them are gifted in different areas. The mountain lion is armed with cunning and strength, the deer with speed and agility. Victory lies in which of the two has a greater *awareness* to their surroundings. This is the same law that determines a Ninja's survival in the spiritual forest. It is not a matter of being stronger or faster, it is a matter of who is more *aware*. Thus, a Ninja should never feel that they must become a hunter in order to survive.

They must simply refine their ability to sense danger and how they respond to it.

THE GUIDANCE OF NATURE

Nature provides the Ninja with all the raw materials needed to cultivate themselves to the highest degree. The forest contains all of the universal elements that serve as the Ninja's teachers. Earth, water, fire and wind. These elements are in total harmony within the forest. It is the Ninja's quest to find such harmony within themselves.

The Four Primary Elements

THE POOL OF KNOWLEDGE

Within the deepest confines of the forest there is a calm pool of water that, although small in size, reflects considerable depth. This pool represents the unlimited amount of information available to those in search of deeper awareness. In essence, the pool is the place where all creatures of the forest come to quench their thirst for knowledge. In reality the pool is the Dojo and the forest is the world that exists around it. The Ninja looks to the pool not only to partake of its life-giving sustenance, but also to see their reflection as they grow with each drink. The pool is the one place in the forest that all creatures have in common. It is a place of gathering, where all animals unite.

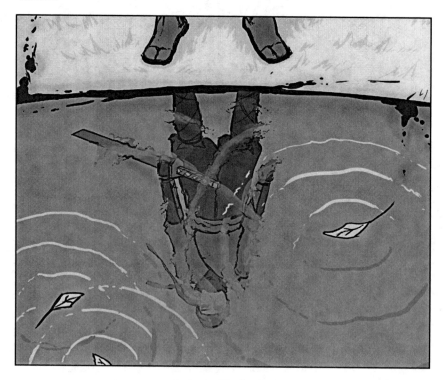

A place of Reflection

THE POWER WITHIN

Within every Ninja there lies a dormant power waiting to emerge. This is the spiritual force on which the Ninja will base all their training. The powers emergence cannot be rushed however. As with all good things, it takes time. To a Ninja this power comes in the form of an animal totem known as a "Bugo," or "Martial Name." These are much more than overly dramatic names given to the Ninja for the sake of ego-posturing. The Ninja receives this name from the Jonin after they have proven themselves worthy of such an honor. Once the Ninja's name has been revealed to them they are entitled to have its likeness committed to their right arm or shoulder with an Irezumi (tattoo). The essence of the tattoo lies in the effect it has on the warrior who wears its design. The tattoo serves as a visual reminder to the Ninja of the importance of their individuality as well as providing a point of focus for the development of their fighting skills.

THE INTERNAL FORGE

The number of adventures available while submerged in the forest's depths are endless. Adventure is where you find it. Only by seizing opportunities as they present themselves can the Ninja prosper. Adventure is another word for "Challenge," but its meaning is very clear. One must explore all feelings — fear, anger, joy, sadness, frustration, love, confusion — these emotions abound in the forest, and it is how the Ninja deals with them that is of importance. Adventuring is a means of application, it is taking the knowledge and insight from the pool and putting it into action in order to gain direct experience.

This is where one finds wisdom. Wisdom is not the sole result of age. Quite to the contrary, it is a trait acquired by surpassing obstacles and using the experience to gain maturity in judgment. To gain experience, however, one must first make the decision to face the challenges that lie before them. This invokes the concept of the

The fire within

"Internal Forge." The forge lies deep within the Ninja's sub-conscious and it represents the overcoming of hesitation. When a challenge presents itself, the Ninja must be prepared to step into the flames of the forge so that they can be tempered by the experience. Entering the forge is a journey to finding the physical, mental and spiritual worth in oneself. For individual Ninja, this test of spirit lasts different amounts of time. Some attune with their internal flames very quickly while others linger. However, time is irrelevant, in the end we must all face ourselves.

THE LAW OF THE WILD

Survival in the forest is difficult at best. Nothing is easy. Although the forest provides a great deal of security, the same forest also inflicts peril. Remember, the forest is neither friend nor foe, but it is capable of harboring both. A Ninja in the forest must be ever vigilant, knowing that today's ally can become tomorrow's enemy. This is the law of the wild. This is a valid philosophy because of the fact that every person must be allowed to live by their own set of morals. One person may not accept another person's method of existence, but conflict is often to no avail. No person should condemn the lifestyle of another. This can be seen in a small part of my own personal philosophy. That philosophy states, "I was not placed on this earth to adhere to the morals of others. Rather I am here to challenge the minds of warriors yet to be. My methods of training are sometimes extreme, but I will never fail to fulfill the dreams that dwell deep in the hearts of those who follow me. I am the epitome of neutrality, capable of anything at anytime." It is because of this knowledge of myself that I am capable of making my students strong. I do what must be done to increase their abilities. I do this by making them face many chaotic situations to test the strength of their physical and mental mettle. Remember, there are two sides to every coin. If you are only capable of remaining strong during favorable times, but falter during those seeming unfavorable, you are only half a warrior. I only hope at some time during their existence every person can get to know themselves in this way so that they will no longer have the need to find fault in others. If one understands and accepts themselves for who they are, they will be able to acknowledge their purpose in the overall picture of life. At this point the person can see the flaw of judging another just because they don't live by the same set of standards. It simply no longer matters what you think or say, everyone must live by their own design.

This type of philosophy takes years to evolve in the Ninja. They must first make the mistake of judging others in the shadow of their own imperfections. Only if the Ninja falls prey to a similar infringement, focused on their own ideals, will the appropriate light be shed to vanquish the shadow in themselves. At this point the parable "Be wary of judging others, lest you wish to be judged," has great meaning.

ONE WARRIOR, ONE ART

The Ninja must have a total belief in the system they study. Over the years I have had many students come to me complaining that the last martial art they studied did not cover all forms of fighting. Some would complain that they never had the opportunity to ground fight, others were distraught that they did not learn weaponry and the list went on. The whole point is that they felt something was missing. Although I am proud that the arts I teach are multi-faceted, I am disappointed that students are so quick to find fault in other systems. It's true that many arts focus on singular aspects of combat, but the true weakness is to pass judgment on them prematurely. All arts teach students a specific way of dealing with opponents. In Karate the main emphasis is on raw power. In Aikido the main focus is on redirecting energy. In Jujutsu the student is taught to control and immobilize. Although this is a limited example, what it illustrates is that each art has its own unique approach to fighting. Many students see these singular approaches as a weakness and attempt to remedy the situation by cross-training in different arts, hoping to gain a wider range of technique. I disagree with this method. It is my experience that the methods and principles maintained by the various styles often clash, making it difficult to truly unite them into a cohesive fighting system. I think a student should think hard before choosing their path, and once chosen, they must be as devout as a priest. In essence, every art can be effective, the practitioner must simply be dedicated long enough to unleash its secrets. Remember, "One warrior, one art." Never confuse yourself. Follow the doctrines of your art with discipline. In the end you will be rewarded.

STAYING FOCUSED

The mind must be kept from wandering, for it is far too easy to stray from the path. One moment we are sure of our purpose and the next we question our entire existence. Such is life. This is why the Ninja must be strong when faced by that which would distract them from their training. If one thing is certain, it is that many things will emerge to interfere. These obstacles are challenges that are set before the Ninja, and if they give in...they are admitting defeat. What it really comes down to is motivation. Although one's teacher is there to guide them on the path, it falls to the student to be motivated to learn. The student must come to know that what they put into the path is what they will get out of it. Thus the most important goal of the student is to stay focused on an objective. That objective is to gather information from their teacher, absorb it, internalize it and perfect it.

THE PURPOSE OF TRAINING

Many times those who walk the path of the warrior ask themselves this question. "Why do I train?" This is a question that could have many answers. However, I believe a student's training is solely based on personal preparation for existence and the potential obstacles they could face along the way. There should be no single focal point. Self-protection, weaponry, strategy, survival, stealth, mysticism. Each of these skills is invaluable so one can adapt to random situations as they occur. This makes coming up with a definitive reason difficult because we cannot be certain what the future holds. In this way, having no purpose is a purpose. This is important because if one trains for a specific reason they sometimes sub-consciously limit themselves to that single objective. However, if one's mind is open and receptive to change, their training will continuously adapt and grow, making the art they study the vehicle used for the attainment of deeper understanding.

SIMPLE PHILOSOPHY

Since I began teaching the way of the Ninja back in the early 1980's, there has been one specific question that has been asked by almost every student. That question is: *What type of philosophy or belief system does the Kurai Kotori Ninja live by?* This is a complex question that contains a myriad of answers, but I will do my best to explain.

First and foremost, a Kurai Kotori Ninja must learn to cultivate themselves in a constructive manner. This can only be accomplished by using one's life experiences to gain insight into how they can better deal with the situations that occur around them. What I mean to say is that there are many perils in life that are inevitable. We can attempt to avoid them, but sooner or later they will catch up to us. We might as well try and receive these experiences with the intent of, for better or worse, using the outcome in a positive manner that promotes growth. _We will make friends and acquire enemies_. _We will find love and learn hatred_. _We will engage in war and cherish peace_. _We will have successes and suffer losses_. _We will live and we will die_. All of these things, and more, will happen during our journey through life. What really matters are the choices we make while journeying. The overall meaning of what I am trying to convey is hidden deep within all of us. The choices we make during the course of our existence have an impact on those around us. The only bit of wisdom I can offer is, "Make a difference." Never just watch on as events unfold, become a part of them.

Many are quick to point out the flaws of the world. Crime, hunger, hatred and corruption. It is true these things exist, but I have a bit of insight for you. It is much easier to sit with your prejudices and avoid change. It is hard to be civil, to listen, to communicate, and to accept that what you learn may change your life. In living this way the student can surpass racism, bigotry, sexism or any other mind altering belief and instead approach life in a constructive manner.

Do not be misguided in any way as to what I am saying. I am not in any way dictating how anyone should live. I am simply pointing out that everyone should have an awareness to the things that are happening around them. The choices they make in life are theirs alone.

MANY PATHS, ONE DESTINATION

Each person who studies a martial art is embarking on a very personal quest that must be respected. Not everyone practices the same style just as not everyone follows the same religion. The Kurai Kotori Ninja must always offer sincere admiration for anyone who practices martial arts, regardless of style or affiliation. Just remember that it is not the style as much as the one who studies it. If they are devout students who practice diligently, that is enough. However, there are those you will meet on the path that are arrogant and boisterous who will claim they are unbeatable, their style is supreme or some other mindless banter.   These braggarts should be avoided because all they are doing is creating unbalanced energy, and thus, bad karma.   If avoidance is not an option, do what you must.

CHAPTER SIX

BODY, MIND,
AND SPIRIT

CHAPTER SIX
BODY, MIND, AND SPIRIT

In the Martial Arts we often hear references to the concept of Body-Mind-Spirit. But what does it really mean? In simplest terms, it represents the unification of our physical, mental and spiritual selves. This unification is sought by warriors in an effort to uncover the mysteries of one's inner self in an attempt to attain some level of personal enlightenment. Although this sounds deep and wise, those who refer to it have very little insight into how to actually attain such unity. The concept is intriguing, but without guidance it has little substance. In the Chronicles of Kurai Kotori there is a guideline that is used to put Body-Mind-Spirit into perspective, diffusing the mystery and providing a pragmatic approach to developing all three aspects.

THE BODY

To begin with, there is the "Body." The body is considered to be the vehicle or receptacle for the inner self. All that you are is contained within this mass. In essence, the body is a temple that houses the mind and spirit. This is a good analogy because if one views their body as a temple, they take care not to defile it in any way. The body temple is to be treated with respect as it is the structure that protects the wisdom that is housed within. The Ninja trains hard to fortify it, to strengthen its outer walls so those who seek to destroy what's within can be repelled effectively. But the outer wall is a shell, the true mysteries lie within. The warrior must enter the gates of the temple if they are to discover the truth of their "inner self."

THE MIND

The "Mind," is the first aspect of our "inner self." The mind is the ultimate expression of what is referred to as "free will." I use this terminology because we are free to think whatever we like, and in turn we are free to make decisions based on those thoughts. However, the wise warrior must not abuse free will by forcing their thoughts on others in a negative fashion. Instead, free will should be expressed in a positive manner that instills growth. If the Ninja allows their negative thoughts to take form in their actions, they only add more pain to a world that is already plagued by various forms of emotional, political, financial and physical enslavement.

THE SPIRIT

Finally, there is the "Spirit." The spirit is the second aspect of our "inner self." It represents a plane of consciousness beyond that of the mind. The spirit, when aware of its strength and power, can influence the mind to make wise choices. When the mind is trained to listen to the spirit, we tend to avoid making painful mistakes, teaching us to be more judicious and not to create negative karmic energy through wrongful actions. Unfortunately, our cultural, educational and sometimes even our religious systems do not spend much time developing this Mind-Spirit connection. Therefore, the mind, which is ruled by the impressions it receives from the external senses (sight, hearing, taste, touch and smell) tends to make choices without consulting the spirit. In essence, the mind reacts prematurely to situations as they occur. This lack of unity between the two is largely responsible for the many stressful situations of everyday life. It was once revealed to me that the mind is a good servant, but a bad master.

RELINQUISHING CONTROL

Through the process of physical training and meditation, the spirit can begin to tame the mind. The Ninja must teach the mind to respect and trust the spirit. This is the only way the spirit can take an active role in our day to day decision making. Once the mind allows the spirit to act as the leader, the Ninja will begin to experience inner-peace. Through meditation, the mind learns how to turn to the spirit's silent inner wisdom for guidance. This is what real free will is all about. The true secret to attaining unity is the subtle connection or bridge between these two powerful entities. We often times pay a high price if we allow the mind to dominate the free will that rightfully belongs to the spirit. If this occurs, the spirit appears to become weaker and weaker in its ability to influence the mind. Fortunately, the spirit cannot truly become weak...it only seems weak...for the spirit is more powerful than the mind because it comes from a higher place, an elevated plane of consciousness. However, the mind can choose to ignore the intuitive strengths of the spirit because they are very subtle, so our connection to it must be cultivated to ensure a unified prosperity.

THE SPIRIT MASTER

In essence, if we can unleash the power of the spirit, we can accomplish anything. The spirit's ability to positively influence our decision making abilities is just the beginning. The spirit holds so much raw energy that it is capable of performing incredible feats. Unfortunately, the spirit is an untapped resource that many warriors ignore on their quest. Those who do search for self-effacement often become more powerful warriors who possess an equal blend of physical skill, mental strength and spiritual peace.

To uncover the essence of Body, Mind, and Spirit, we must focus on each of them as singular entities while at the same time acknowledging that they are interwoven.

CHAPTER SEVEN

PHYSICAL
PREPARATION

CHAPTER SEVEN
PHYSICAL PREPARATION

Five areas of physical skill are required to become an effective Ninja. Strength, Endurance, Flexibility, Balance, and Agility. The body must undergo rigorous training to maximize the efficiency of these attributes.

STRENGTH DRILLS

The building of physical toughness in an effort to increase one's ability to deliver and resist force. Strength training should be a compliment not an impediment. This means that one must not increase muscle mass at the cost of flexibility or speed. But strong, healthy muscles can create explosive strength, which is the kind of strength sought by a Ninja.

MAKIWARA

One of the most overlooked aspects of strength training is daily makiwara practice. Makiwara are "Striking targets" used to condition the hands and feet to deliver maximum damage. A makiwara can take many forms. A plank of wood buried in the ground with its upper end wrapped in slim padding, a wall mounted target covered in padding and canvas, or even a thick trunk of wood with thin padded targets on its surface.

Makiwara Design

STRIKING THE MAKIWARA

The main method of makiwara conditioning is applied with the clenched fist (striking with the two upper-most knuckles) and the toe strike (striking with the ball of the foot). These are the two most powerful body weapons used in thrusting attacks. However, other body weapons (elbows, knees, head) can also be conditioned by striking the makiwara board. Consistent practice has developed punches that registered close to 2000 lbs. per square inch, which is as high as humanly possible. An extended sequence of repetitious practice conditions the muscles of the body to receive the shock of an impact. This builds strength, power and kime (focused energy). For a Ninja it is mandatory to hit the makiwara 50 times per hand, per training session. This practice inspires the practitioner to fully commit to each punch.

MUSHIN

Makiwara training also develops mushin, which is most commonly translated as "no mind." "Mu" meaning negation, "Shin" meaning heart, mind, feeling. No mind is a Zen term referring to that state of mental clarity and enhanced perception (sensory and intuitive) also known as "pure mind," produced by the absence of conscious thought, ideas, judgments, emotion (fear and anxiety), pre-conception, or self-consciousness. For the Ninja, meditation (towards mushin) is an important compliment to technical training. Through mushin the mind is not absent, it is free. No longer inhibited, slowed, distracted, or clogged, the mind is free to fully perceive, respond and commit to action. The mind is not fixed on anything and is open to everything; a mind expanded through the whole body with total awareness of and focus on everything.

Striking the Makiwara

HORIZONTAL POLE

The horizontal pole is invaluable in a Ninja's strength training and there are a variety of exercises using poles of different heights.

HANGING

First and foremost, the Ninja can hang by the hands with palms forward to condition the arms and shoulders. To increase the challenge, small bags of sand can be placed over the shoulders like saddlebags. The goal - Hang as long as possible without touching the feet to the ground. The Ninja can also hang upside down by folding the legs over the pole and allowing the body to hang down with arms extended. Although this is a strength drill, it is also an effective endurance drill.

Hanging from a Horizontal Pole

PULL UPS

Pull ups can be performed with palms inward and outward and with both two hands and single hands. This is great training for the arms, shoulders and back muscles. This exercise can also be applied by placing small rope loops on the pole that the wrists can be placed in, allowing the biceps to receive the primary attention.

Pull ups on a Horizontal Pole

DIPS

Pushing upward off of vertical posts is very effective for conditioning the chest and triceps.

Dips between two objects

ELEVATED PUSH UPS

Executing push ups by placing the feet on a slightly elevated object allows the Ninja to enhance the overall effectiveness of a traditional push up. This works the chest as well as the shoulders and triceps. To increase the workout, the Ninja can practice the push up on the fore knuckles or finger tips to condition their striking weapons. The most rigorous version of the exercise is done on the ridge hand with the arms spread further apart.

Elevated push ups on an object

RECEIVING IMPACTS

Physical toughness when taking a hit is just as important, if not more so, than delivering a powerful strike. In combat, the Ninja must close range to deliver an attack, and in doing so must enter into the striking range of their opponent. This critical range is where attacks and counterattacks will move with furious speed...and in that situation the possibility of being struck is almost guaranteed. Thus, the limbs and torso must be conditioned to absorb these impacts. This is accomplished a variety of ways.

BAMBOO SWORD

First and foremost is taking repeated strikes against the shins and forearms with a chikuto (bamboo sword). These impacts do not have to be full force, but should provide a significant amount of energy in an effort to condition the body's natural shields.

Absorbing strikes from a bamboo sword

ABSORBING KICKS

The torso and legs should be conditioned by receiving circular and thrusting kicks. Emphasis should be on learning to properly adjust the position of the body to effectively absorb the energy in the larger muscles. Although physical strength is important, it should also be noted that proper breathing is imperative when taking a hit because although the body is contracted, air must flow unhindered to keep a bit of pliability to assist in dispersing the incoming energy.

Absorbing kicks to the body

ENDURANCE DRILLS

Endurance drills are designed to maximize the Ninja's ability to withstand physical hardship for extended periods of time. Physical stamina can be developed through specific exercises combined with proper breathing technique.

STRADDLE LEG POSITION

Leg strength and pliability in the hips. This core flexibility is perhaps the most important overall. A Ninja may have to climb, stay low while moving, or remain concealed for an extended period of time. It is important that the thighs are horizontal and the back is straight during this exercise as dropping too low in the straddle negates the positive effects.

Straddle leg position

CLAY POTS

Holding the arms out the sides while gripping the mouth of a clay pot puts stress on the shoulders and limbs while at the same time enhancing grip strength. The pots are filled with varying amounts of sand or clay to increase the weight to accommodate the needs of the specific Ninja using them. The goal of the exercise is to hold the pots as long as possible without dropping the arms or allowing the grip to falter. This exercise can be combined with the straddle leg position to increase the complexity level. Beyond the first position, the pots can also be held extended sideways or turned upward to change the distribution of energy, which will put stress on different muscles in the forearms and shoulders.

Gripping clay pots

WRINGING CLOTH

To build forearm endurance and twisting strength the Ninja uses a large cloth soaked in water. Counter twisting pressure is applied to the cloth to wring the water out. The cloth is twisted until no water remains. The cloth is then dipped in water again and the process repeated.

Wringing water from a cloth

JUMP LUNGES

Leg and hip conditioning require a rigorous amount of work that can be accomplished with jump lunges.

Alternating Jump Lunges

FLEXIBILITY DRILLS

When the concept of flexibility is brought up, the first thought is usually about leg splits. However, the act of stretching refers to increasing the body's pliability when turned, bowed, or twisted. This means that every joint and bend in the body should be conditioned to a point where they become supple and less prone to injury.

SHOULDERS

Shoulder stretches can be applied by placing the right hand on the left shoulder while using the left hand to pull the right elbow further to the left. This exercise should be done with both arms and followed by small circle rotations with both shoulders.

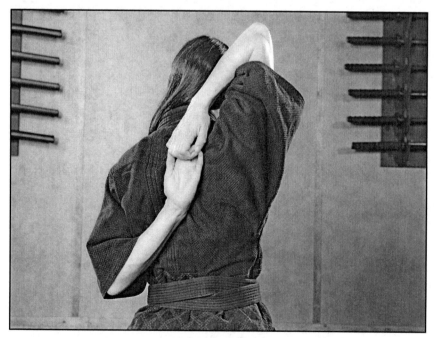

Shoulder flexibility

WRISTS

Wrists should be stretched by placing hands palm to palm, keeping them together while applying downward pressure in front of the body. Next, the wrists should be twisted palm outward while applying pressure to back of the hand with the opposite hand.

Wrist flexibility

BACK

The back is stretched by laying face down while extending the torso up by extending the arms while keeping the hips flat against the ground. Then from a seated position, the right leg is extended outward with the left leg retracted and placed over the right knee. The right arm is placed on the outside of the left knee as the left arm twists to the rear.

Back flexibility

HIPS

Starting in a leg lunge position with the left leg forward, the left arm is placed under the left knee, focusing on pushing the chest toward the ground. Then a seated position with bottoms of the feet together is assumed. The feet are pulled inward with the hands while the elbows are used to apply downward pressure to the legs.

Hip flexibility

LEGS

A side lunge is assumed with the left leg extended while the right leg is placed bent beneath the torso. Subtle pressure is applied by leaning into the stretch. The position is alternated. Next, one foot is placed in a rope loop that is attached to a pulley. The rope is then pulled with the hands until the leg is in a comfortable stretch.

Leg flexibility

BALANCE DRILLS

The ability to move or remain in a specific position without losing control and falling.

HANDSTAND BALANCE

The hands are placed on the ground with the feet extended upward with a slight bend in the knees.

Balancing on the hands

PILLAR BALANCE

Balancing on one foot while standing on a raised object for a ten count. At the end of the count the legs are switched by hopping upward and alternating the foot positions.

Balancing on a single pillar

BALANCE ON BEAM

Walking forward and backward on a horizontal beam will enhance centerline balance. To increase difficulty, one can jump upward, turn the body in mid air, and drop back onto the beam facing the opposite direction.

Balancing on a beam

AGILITY DRILLS

Agility is the Ninja's ability to explosively brake, change direction and accelerate again.

SLOPING WALL

Running up a deeply angled wall will increase one's ability to alter and control body weight and momentum.

Running up an angled surface

LEAPING UPWARD

Leaping up onto an object will increase the ability to gauge the amount of energy needed to propel the body into the air and land delicately on a raised platform. This is also highly effective as an endurance exercise.

Jumping onto an elevated object

JUMPING DOWNWARD

Descending with a leap is all about jumping upward and outward at the same time so the body can drop straight down rather than angular. The landing energy needs to be dispersed equally between the hips, knees, and ankles. The landing can move directly into a roll to further disperse energy.

Jumping off an elevated object

AVOIDING PROJECTILES

The ability to instinctively and accurately propel the body in a desired direction is imperative. Avoiding thrown projectiles increases this skill by learning to assess the trajectory of the object at a moments notice and avoiding its impact.

Avoiding thrown objects

ENDLESS ALTERNATIVES

There are countless exercises beyond those shown in this book. What is important is that the Ninja remain focused on the continued development of their body temple. The specific exercises can change, but the effect is the same.

CHAPTER EIGHT

MENTAL
PREPARATION

CHAPTER EIGHT
MENTAL PREPARATION

Although the concept of meditation is difficult for many westerners to embrace, it is the key to unifying the body, mind, and spirit. Meditation strengthens and enhances the Ninja's natural intuitive wisdom, which is valuable in all areas of life. In the simplest possible terms, meditation can be seen as "reflection," the ability to stop and analyze what's happening around you, or "contemplation" about something that is important in your life.

THE ELEMENTS WITHIN

Since the five elements of nature are so prevalent in the Ninja's overall thought process, it is no surprise that this same dynamic is present as a meditative process, using the elements to identify power centers that exist within all living creatures. Earth, Water, Fire, Wind and Celestial. These elements provide insightful reflection into the depth of our very being. By focusing on a specific element, we enable ourselves to connect with various parts of our consciousness. In essence, each of the elements gives the Ninja a practical view into the multi-faceted nature of their physical, emotional and spiritual being.

Elemental meditation is extremely indepth. Each of the individual elements offer a vast array of hidden lessons that a diligent Ninja will find only after prolonged study.

Each of the five levels of elemental meditation utilize a specific thought process and a variety of unique implements to enhance the experience. It is important that the Ninja become proficient with one element before moving on to the next. They are like building blocks, each one serving as the foundation for the next. They are not separate, but rather a continuous path that leads to a greater understanding of self.

The elements within

ACKNOWLEDGING THE POWER CENTERS

There are five primary power centers. Each one referring to one of the elements. These are the powerful energies that bind everything in existence together. They can be seen on a large scale in the very world we live in. We have land masses (earth), vast oceans (water), a molten core (fire), an atmosphere (wind), and we are held aloft in space (celestial). Our bodies harness the same energies. We have bones and muscles (earth), ever flowing blood (water), we emanate heat (fire), we breathe (wind) and we have our mind and spirit (celestial). Take even one of these elements out of the equation...and we cease to exist. Thus, we must come to the conclusion that all of these furies must be maintained if we are to thrive.

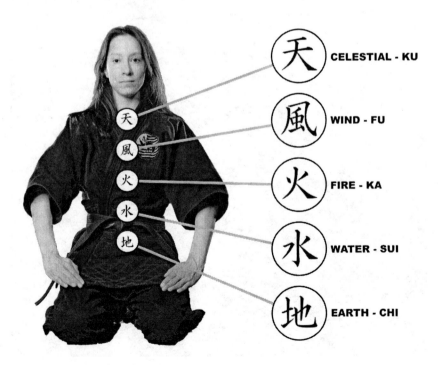

Energy points

THE POSTURE

When a Ninja meditates they should assume the "Fudoza" posture with the legs crossed and the back straight. If the posture is done correctly, the Ninja should feel very stable as though they are made of stone. This feeling is known as "Fudotai," the Immovable Body. Not only must the body remain strong and focused, the mind must as well. To do this the Ninja must focus on their "Seika no itten," or "Vital point" located at their center. This area is where the mind and body can attain unity.

Fudoza no kamae

THE POWER OF BREATHING

Once the Ninja has assumed a proper Fudoza position and they have put their focus on attuning with the center of their being they can move on to rhythmic breathing. Long breaths traveling deep within the body are necessary. As air travels into the Ninja they must concentrate on flooding their vital point with oxygen. This form of breathing is more effective than taking shallow breaths that stop in the chest. As the intake of air continues, the Ninja should concentrate on slowing their breathing, making each breath last as long as possible. Slowly inhaling, slowly exhaling. Breathing may appear to be a rather mundane thing to do, but in actuality, it is the first form of meditation. If the Ninja concentrates on the breath as it floods their system and is then expelled in a controlled fashion it is quite mesmerizing. If this is done in relative seclusion, with no outside interruptions, the Ninja can use breathing to relax and relieve stress. What is important is the concept of "Naga Iki" or "Long Breath, Long Life." This implies that all living creatures have a predestined number of breaths before they die. If they are wasted by breathing shallow and fast, life ends sooner. If breaths are controlled and calm, life lasts longer. The equation is simple.

Long life

209

THE FIRST POWER CENTER

Studying the individual power centers begins with the Seika No Itten (abdomen). This power center is located at the base of the spine at the tailbone in back, and the pubic bone in front. This power center holds the basic needs for survival, security and safety. The Seika No Itten is powerfully related to our contact with the Earth plane. This is also the center of physical manifestation. When you are trying to make things happen in the material world, the initial energy to succeed will come from the first power center. If the Seika No Itten is blocked, the Ninja may feel fearful, anxious, insecure and frustrated.

Seika no itten

EARTH MEDITATION

The Ninja sits in Fudoza and assumes the Chi-No-In handsign by placing the little finger against the tip of the thumb, forming a circle. The hands are then joined together by linking the circles together like a chain. The hands are then placed softly in the lap. The Ninja then begins their breathing exercises. Focus should be on centering energy in the hip area. After a few minutes, the Ninja should concentrate on the sensation of all the bones and muscles of their body, attempting to attune with the earth element within themselves.

Chi-no-in

211

EARTH VISUALIZATION

Feel where you body meets the floor. Allow it to sink, to attune with the ground itself. Become aware of every aspect of your physical form, your head to your toes. The weight of your torso, the heaviness of your limbs. Now, focus on the lower abdomen, extending through the body to the tailbone. This is your earth power center. The Seika no Itten.

Its energy is red and it swirls in a circular glory. This energy governs your physical body, your health, your vitality. In your mind, study the appearance of the earth power center, note its color, allow it to swell. Mentally probe your body for any symptoms of lapsing health. Have you been caring for your body temple? Are you aware of any ailments hindering you? Allow the energy of the **SEIKA NO ITTEN** *to wash over these impurities, cleanse them, repair them.*

Now, return your attention to the earth power center. It is clean and bright red. You are illuminated in the energy of Earth. Imagine the room glowing red with this energy, feel its sheer strength, allow the energy to swirl and flow to your earth power center. In your mind you can see your earth center, a brilliant red swirling vortex of physical energy.

THE SECOND POWER CENTER

The second power center is the Hara (stomach). This power center is located just above the navel. This center holds the basic needs for sexuality and creative expression. This power center is also about strong emotions and intuition, which is directly related to the Water plane. The Hara governs one's sense of self-worth and their ability to relate to others in an open and friendly way. Proper balance in this power center means one has the ability to flow with emotions freely. If the Hara is blocked, the Ninja may feel emotionally explosive, manipulative, obsessed, or may lack energy.

Hara

WATER MEDITATION

The Ninja sits in Fudoza and assumes the Sui-No-In handsign by placing the second finger against the tip of the thumb, forming a circle. The hands are then joined together by linking the circles together like a chain. The hands are then placed softly in the lap. The Ninja then begins their breathing exercises. Focus should be on centering energy in the lower stomach. After a few minutes, the Ninja should concentrate on the sensation of the blood that flows through their body, attempting to attune with the water element within themselves.

Sui-no-in

WATER VISUALIZATION

Become aware of your blood as it circulates through you, the constant flow. Never-ending movement. Relentless in its duty to sustain the body.

Allow your focus to rise from the earth power center (abdomen) to the stomach, extending through the body to the spine. This is your water power center, the Hara.

*Its energy is orange and it radiates tremendous power. This energy controls clear thinking and creativity. Study the appearance of the water power center, note its color, allow it to swell. Probe your mind. Are your thoughts easily accessed? Is your mind a jumble with activity? Allow the energy of the **HARA** to wash over your mind, organize your thoughts. Put everything in order, allow your mind to easily access the infinite amount of information stored within you.*

Now, return your attention to the water power center. It is clean and radiant orange. You are illuminated in the energy of Water. See the energy as it expands, charging you with creative vitality, until you are bathed in its luminescence. In your mind you can see the water center, a powerful orange vortex of clear unbridled thought.

THE THIRD POWER CENTER

The third power center is referred to as the Suigetsu (solar plexus). It is located two inches below the breastbone in the center behind the stomach. The Suigetsu is the center of personal power, the place of ego, of passions, impulses, anger and strength, all of which is tied to the Fire plane. This is also the center for astral travel and astral influences, receptivity of spirit guides and for psychic development. When this power center is balanced, one is outgoing, has self-respect, is expressive, and enjoys taking on new challenges. When the third power center is out of balance the Ninja may lack confidence, be confused, worry about what others think, feel that others are controlling their life, or may become depressed.

Suigetsu

FIRE MEDITATION

The Ninja sits in Fudoza and assumes the Ka-No-In handsign by placing the middle finger against the tip of the thumb, forming a circle. The hands are then joined together by linking the circles together like a chain. The hands are then placed softly in the lap. The Ninja then begins their breathing exercises. Focus should be on centering energy in the solar plexus. After a few minutes, the Ninja should concentrate on the sensation of all the heat in their body, attempting to attune with the fire element within themselves.

Ka-no-in

FIRE VISUALIZATION

Become aware of the heat that emanates from your body, the unseen energy that radiates ever-vigilant warmth.

Allow your focus to rise from the water power center (stomach) and up to the Solar Plexus. This is your fire power center. The Suigetsu.

Its energy glows radiant yellow and it projects immense force.

*This energy oversees your will and ambition. Embrace this energy. Reach out and sense any impurities. Have you been lazy? Or perhaps you are just not driven lately. Allow the energy of the **SUIGETSU** to engulf these flaws to re-focus your mind.*

Now, return your attention to the fire power center. It is clean and bright yellow. You are bathed in the radiant energy of Fire. The energy expands until it surrounds you, giving you the ability to strive ever forward, working towards what you value and desire. In your mind you can see the fire center, a warm yellow vortex of endless passion.

THE FOURTH POWER CENTER

The fourth power center is referred to as the Kokoro (heart). It is located behind the breast bone in front and on the spine between the shoulder blades in back. The Kokoro is the center for love, compassion and spirituality. This center directs one's ability to love themselves and others, which is directly related to the Wind plane. The Kokoro connects the body and mind with the spirit. Proper balance in this power center allows the Ninja to feel compassionate, friendly, empathetic, and creates the desire to nurture others. If the Kokoro is blocked, the Ninja may feel sorry for themselves, paranoid, indecisive, afraid of letting go, afraid of getting hurt, or unworthy of love.

Kokoro

WIND MEDITATION

The Ninja sits in Fudoza and assumes the Fu-No-In handsign by placing the pointer finger against the tip of the thumb, forming a circle. The hands are then joined together by linking the circles together like a chain. The hands are then placed softly in the lap. The Ninja then begins their breathing exercises. Focus should be on centering energy in the chest area. After a few minutes, the Ninja should concentrate on the sensation of all the air in their body, attempting to attune with the wind element within themselves.

Fu-no-in

WIND VISUALIZATION

Become aware of the air that travels through your body...the invisible energy that fills your lungs.

Allow your focus to rise from the fire power center (solar plexus) to the chest. This is your wind power center. The Kokoro.

Its energy is green and it radiates a gentle softness. This energy governs your feelings, your emotional connections to others, to the universe, to life itself. Reflect a moment on how you've been feeling lately. Are there bindings holding in emotional pain? Allow the energy of the **KOKORO** to capture and release any tensions, imperfections or impurities.

Now, return your attention to the wind power center. It is a clean, beautiful green color. You are bathed in the radiant energy of Wind. It rushes through you strongly and evenly. Open your heart to the world, to all beings big and small, with compassion for our shared journey through life. Feel the green energy whirling into your heart. Watch the power center grow and spin with this new positive energy.

THE FIFTH POWER CENTER

The fifth power center is referred to as the Koka (throat). It is located in the V of the collarbone at the lower neck and is the center of communication, sound, and expression of creativity via thought, speech, and writing. The possibility for change, transformation and healing are located here, invoked by the power of the spoken word. When this power center is balanced the Ninja feels centered, inspired artistically, and they are able to effectively convey thoughts to others. When this power center is out of balance the Ninja wants to hold back, may feel timid, remain quiet, or feel weak, unable to find a way to effectively express their thoughts.

Koka

CELESTIAL MEDITATION

The Ninja then assumes the Ku-No-In handsign by placing the left palm on top of the right palm and touching the thumbs together. The hands are then placed softly in the lap. The Ninja then begins their breathing exercises. Focus should be on centering their energy in the throat. After a few minutes, the Ninja should concentrate on harnessing spiritual energy, attempting to attune with the celestial element within themselves.

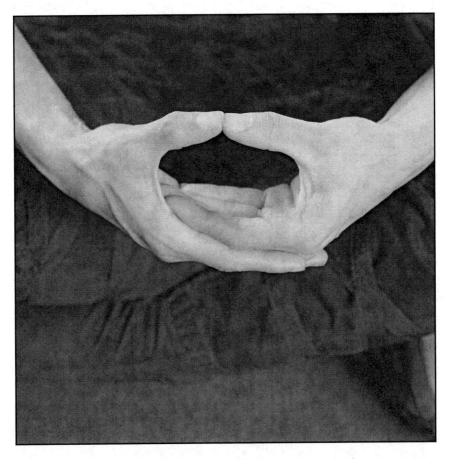

Ku-no-in

CELESTIAL VISUALIZATION

Become aware of your voice, the power the spoken word. The invisible force capable of a soft whisper or a resonating scream.

Allow your focus to rise from the wind power center (chest) to settle in the throat. This is your celestial power center. The Koka.

Its energy is blue and it emits a soothing sound. This energy governs communication and personal magnetism. Study the appearance of the celestial power center. Reach out and sense any imperfections. Perhaps you haven't been honoring your own beliefs and speaking out when you should. Or perhaps you've been talking over others, or not listening well. Maybe you've been feeling shy, afraid to extend your energy into positive communication. Allow the energy of the KOKA to erupt and destroy these impurities.

Now, return your attention to the celestial power center. It is a clean, strong, and bright blue. See it fill up with Celestial energy. Feel the throat open as this energy expands. The energy charges your aura with magnetism, drawing others to you.

In your mind, you can see the celestial power center. A spiritual force that surrounds all that you are.

CHAPTER NINE

SPIRITUAL
PREPARATION

CHAPTER NINE
SPIRITUAL PREPARATION

A Ninja must be ready to face death at any moment. No fear. No regrets. A Ninja knows that in order to be truly free, they must live each day in an honest attempt to reach their goals. Even if these goals were not fully achieved before the last breath falls from their lips, the Ninja can die knowing that they were devout in their quest.

Death is such a frightening word, but in reality it is simply the end of a life cycle. Whether you believe that there is another phase of existence waiting for us after we pass, believe we will be reincarnated, or that when life ends... it ends, all beliefs come from whatever religious doctrines we have been exposed to during our lives.

Classical Japanese Ninja were exposed to many beliefs throughout the centuries. Shinto, Buddhism, Mikkyo, Taoism, Shugendo, Onmyodo, Koshin, Confucianism, Christianity, and many other religious paths that provided insights into the inner workings of the universe. Seeking answers from any of these resources, then or now, is based on faith... and such conviction differs from person to person.

But what about spirituality beyond religion? Spirituality is about finding a connection to that part of ourselves that allows us to feel whole, vibrant, and blissful.

What is it that fulfils the soul while we exist in this phase of life? What is it we each seek? Deep within all of us we have something, or sometimes multiple things, that make us feel at peace. A writer *needs* to put pen to paper, a dancer *needs* to move in rhythmic fashion, a musician *needs* to play or sing, and an actor *needs* to perform. These and a multitude of other possibilities exist within all of us. A deep seeded *need* to do something. Because these needs do not always fit within the spectrum of what many would deem important to a successful life, they are often discarded as fanciful rather than practical. Nothing could be farther from the truth. The ability to create is a very spiritual aspect of our existence.

An actor needs to perform

How often do we hear people reminisce on an earlier aspect of their lives with a somber reflection that they are no longer doing one or more of those things that at one time truly fulfilled them. The painting they used to do, the poetry they used to write. But since these things are difficult to maintain in a world where monetary success seemingly overshadows all, they were pushed back deep in the recesses of the mind. A fond memory of things that might have been.

These soul-soothing aspects of our lives may not be religious in nature, but they are, without a doubt, spiritual. Things that represent the energy we carry inside us and the desire to let it emerge. Thus, to hold it in, deny it an outlet, or even convince ourselves it is not important in the grander scheme of life is the one choice that will hamper our connection to our spiritual freedom.

Although this seems like a simple concept, to truly pursue one's spiritual expression with full intensity is a difficult process. The world is filled with distractions and events that will seek to take us from our desired path. Life will bombard us with many situations that will be both gift and burden. Whether these be in the form of opportunity, tragedy, gain, or loss is not what's important. It's how we use any or all of these things to propel us ever forward toward our chosen objectives.

What will inevitably happen is that these life events will have subtle influences, both positive and negative, that will affect change. Change is growth, but these changes often take us away from our spiritual expressions rather than toward them. Although a positive life event may provide an opportunity for financial expansion, it may come at the cost of ultimate happiness because it alters one's spiritual course.

Looking back at our youth and remembering the honesty and marvel with which we envisioned our future lives. Anything seemed possible because our imaginations were not tainted by the reality of life. These may not have been fully informed choices, but the one thing that was evident is that we *believed*.

Although there are many approaches to spiritual refinement, the Kurai Kotori Ninja are encouraged to start with finding an artistic expression that fulfils them. No matter what it is, the creation of something from nothing is an amazing transformation.

Spirituality through art is something that is very evident in Japanese culture. Calligraphy (shodo), tea ceremony (chanoyu), pottery (kakiemon), flower arranging (ikebana), picture scrolls (e-makimono) paintings on wooden doors (Raigo), woodblock prints (ukiyo-e), performing arts (noh, kabuki, bunraku, chambara), and poetry (tanka, haiku), all have spiritual components in their application.

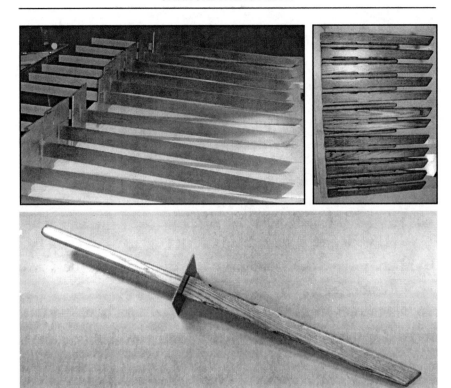

The author designs and constructs custom shinobigatana

Practicing Shodo

UNDERSTANDING DUALITY

There is no way to create a 100% positive life, but there is a way to create a 100% negative one. The true answer lies in knowing that you can never allow the darkness to consume the light. Sacrifices will always have to be made, suffering will need to be endured, and obstacles will have to be conquered. Light and shadow cannot exist without one another. This simple yet profound observation tells us that we are part of a grander scheme that bombards us with both positive and negative forces. It falls to us to seize the right moments, do what must be done, make the hard choices, and all with the knowledge that we will lose some battles in our effort to win the war. There is no perfect answer to making everything work positively without flaw, which is possibly the truest thing I could ever write. The happily ever after vision of following one's dreams along with the concept that all those dreams will come true is indeed possible... yet improbable... unless there are significant sacrifices. The balance of nature cannot be denied. Thus it is important that when we are lamenting about the hardships we've faced, the losses we've endured, the loneliness we've suffered... just know that if this adversity is faced in an effort to take us to a desired goal, then the trials and tribulations will be worth it. But if these misfortunes are used as excuses as to why we have failed, or cannot hope to succeed, then we will succumb to the darkness in the form of mediocrity and self immolation. In essence the understanding that death is ever present is a strong motivator to pursue your passions and live each day to its fullest. Find your Bliss. - *Mark Steven Grove*